ELECTORAL SECURITY FRAMEWORK

TECHNICAL GUIDANCE HANDBOOK FOR DEMOCRACY AND GOVERNANCE OFFICERS

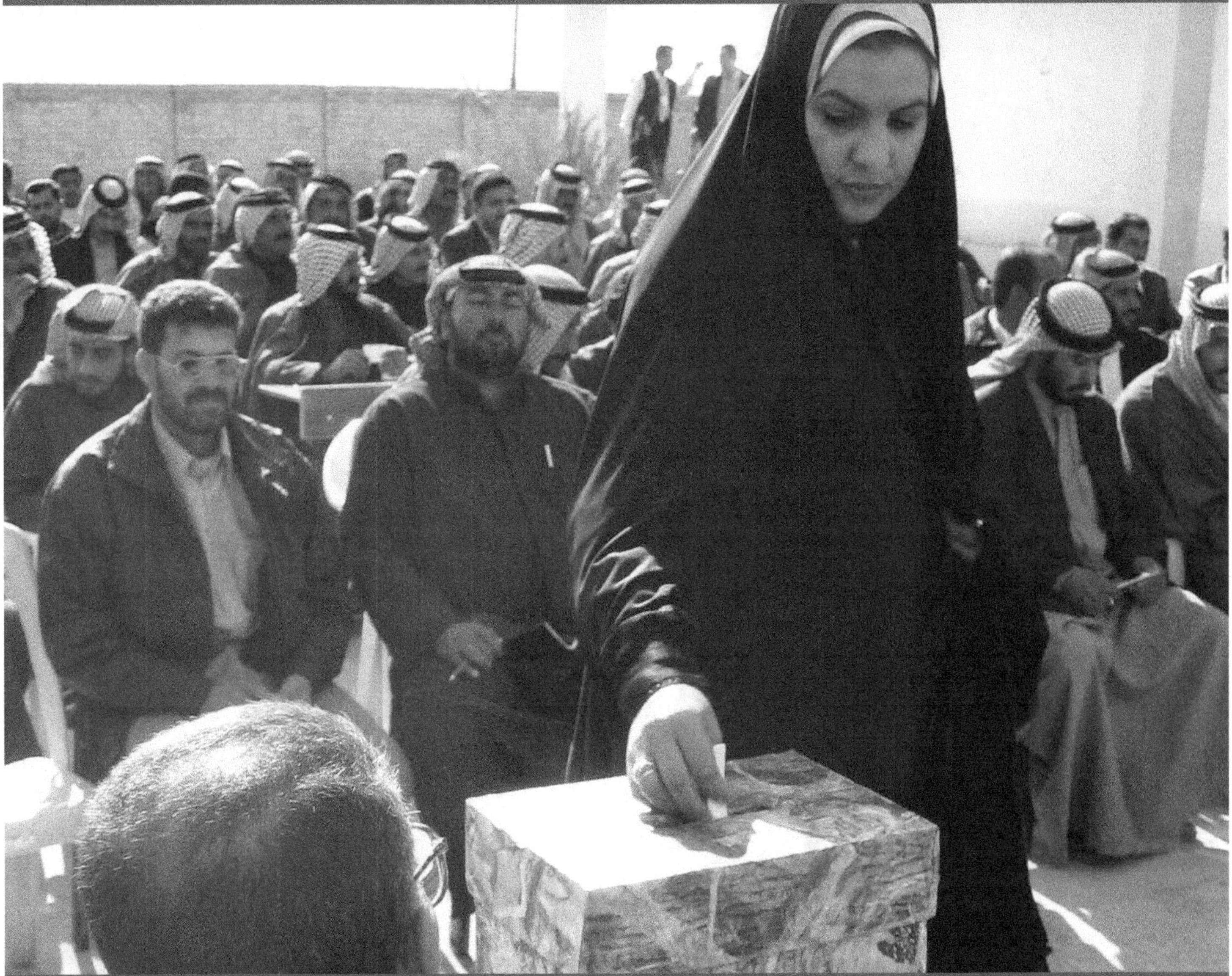

JULY 2010

This report was produced for review by the United States Agency for International Development. It was prepared by Creative Associates International, Inc. The author's views expressed in this publication do not necessarily reflect the views of the United States Agency for International Development (USAID) or the United States Government.

TABLE OF CONTENTS

TABLES AND FIGURES

ANNEXES

ACKNOWLEDGEMENTS

The Electoral Security Framework was written by Creative Associates International, Inc. (Creative) under funding from the United States Agency for International Development (USAID). Jeff Fischer, Karen Kaplan and Elisabeth Bond completed the Framework with great help from fellow Creative colleagues Jeffrey Carlson, Patrick Quirk, Luis Aguilar, and Marta Maldonado. Supporting research was compiled by Yume Kitasei. The opinions and observations expressed in this document are those of the authors. They are not necessarily the views of the United States Government or USAID.

The authors wish to thank committed colleagues from international agencies who generously provided key informant interviews, shared documents and gave of their time to discuss the Framework. In particular, the authors are grateful for the insights provided by local institutions and USAID missions in Bangladesh, Colombia, and Zimbabwe. In particular, Adam Schumacher (Acting Director, Office of Democracy and Governance) and Lazhar Aloui in Bangladesh; Jene Thomas (Director, Office of Democracy and Human Rights), Paula Cobo, Lucia Garcia, and Lucy Malo in Colombia; and Kevin Sturr (Team Leader) and Otto Saki in Zimbabwe. Additionally, we thank Mary T. An, United Nations Development Programme (UNDP); Eric Beinhart, International Criminal Investigation Assistance Program (ICITAP); Dorina Bekoe, US Institute for Peace (USIP); Pete Dordal, Garda World Security; Peter Erben, International Foundation for Electoral Systems (IFES); Anne Gloor, Swiss Federal Department of Foreign Affairs (FDFA); and Michael Maley, Australian Election Commission (AEC) for their review of and contributions to the document.

Many thanks are given to those USAID Officers who attended the initial Participant Training in May 2010, and those individuals who participated in the January 2010 Workshop on Electoral Security: Strategies for Policy and Practice. Attendees, all extremely knowledgeable in the fields of elections and security, provided insightful comments and concrete guidance to USAID and Creative on the development of the Assessment Framework and Training. Thank you to the following individuals for their timely and constructive review of the Framework: Spencer Abbot, USAID; Gabrielle Bardall, IFES; Angela Bargellini, UN Electoral Assistance Division (UNEAD); Tihana Bartulac-Blanc, American University, Center for Democracy and Election Management (CDEM); Eric Bjornlund, Democracy International; Glenn Cowan, Democracy International; Dave Davis, George Mason University, Peace Operations; Pete Dordal, Garda World Security; Phil Figgins, Pax Mondial; Lisa Handley; Geoff Hughes, IFES; Cate Johnson, USAID; Edward Joseph, US Helsinki Commission; William Lafontaine, US Department of Defense; Marissa LeMargie, USAID; Terrence Lyons, George Mason University, Institute for Conflict Analysis and Resolution (ICAR); Elizabeth Martin, USAID; Amy Mawson, Princeton University; Greg Minjack, USAID; Matthew Pilcher, Global Strategies Group; Tom Pope, USAID; Brian Stout, USAID; Michael D. Svetlik, IFES; Dorothy Douglas Taft, USAID; Chad Vickery, IFES; Barry H. Weinberg, US Department of Justice, (Ret.); Julie Werbel, USAID; and Paul Wood, Pax Mondial.

Finally, the Handbook authors would like to recognize and thank Tess McEnery, Carrie Gruenloh, and Mike Henning of USAID's Democracy and Governance - Elections and Political Processes (DG/EPP) Team. Their dedication to this initiative demonstrates EPP's commitment to improved programming in the fields of electoral integrity and security. Without their efforts, the Electoral Security Framework would not have been possible.

EXECUTIVE SUMMARY

Man displays inked finger after voting in the July 2009 Indonesian Presidential Election.

Electoral conflict remains an obstacle to the consolidation of democratic institutions for many countries. Even in stable political environments, elections can fall victim to conflict. Although a problem that is global in scope, electoral conflict and its root causes, profiles and intensities differ in each country context. If development programming is not undertaken to prevent, manage or mediate electoral conflict, then elections risk becoming venues for violence and intimidation, where conflict is employed as a political tactic to influence electoral outcomes. The importance of this issue extends beyond the electoral process alone, as the legitimacy of the resulting government is also at risk in situations where conflict has been employed to achieve governance. Perpetrators of electoral conflict may act without legal consequences, engendering a culture of impunity for such crimes. Recurring elec-

toral conflict can create public perceptions that link elections to violence, leading to unfavorable views of the democratic process. Electoral conflict can also have regional implications, as internal conflicts might spill into neighboring countries.

Electoral conflict is an issue that bridges two development portfolios at the United States Agency for International Development (USAID) – Elections and Political Processes (EPP) and Conflict Management and Mitigation (CMM). As such, it poses unique programming challenges for USAID in its effort to coordinate these two development priorities. The Electoral Security Framework (the Framework) presented in this Technical Guidance Handbook reflects a blended perspective of the USAID Democracy and Governance Assessment Framework,

USAID's Conflict Assessment Framework (CAF) and the Interagency Conflict Assessment Framework (ICAF). The Electoral Security Framework presents analytical concepts intended to be compatible with these existing USAID Frameworks while also distinctively addressing electoral conflict. The Framework can be used on either side of this complex set of development issues - bringing a conflict dimension to electoral assistance programming or an electoral dimension to conflict management and mitigation. The Framework is relevant for and should be used by practitioners on either side.

The Framework aims to fill what has been described as a "yawning gap of knowledge about how programming can more consistently and effectively address the causes, manifestations, and consequences of election violence."[1]

The Framework is a diagnostic instrument that profiles electoral conflict for the development of program strategies and activities to prevent, manage or mediate this conflict. As such, it is applicable in two different kinds of scenarios: otherwise stable environments where elections may trigger conflict (i.e. Bangladesh); and conflict or post-conflict environments (i.e. Sudan). The purpose of this Handbook is to provide USAID Democracy and Governance (DG) Officers with a guide to the Framework and its application for the development of sustainable electoral security systems.

This Handbook is organized around the following Framework components: 1) Electoral Security Assessment; 2) Electoral Security Planning; 3) Electoral Security Programming; and 4) Monitoring and Evaluation. The entire Framework is made actionable in the final section through the Electoral Security Toolkit.

ELECTORAL SECURITY ASSESSMENT

The electoral security assessment is conducted using both a desk study and information gathering in the field. The assessment is composed of three chief areas of analysis.

- **Contextual Analysis:** What are the electoral conflict risk factors found in the security, political, economic, social and public administrative sectors? What other risk factors—such as the type of electoral or political party system—exist?

- **Historical Conflict factors:** Has there been conflict surrounding past elections?

- **State and Non-state Stakeholders:** What are the characteristics of these stakeholders,

and how do they relate to electoral security? Information gathered through the historical and contextual analysis can be applied to stakeholder analysis to determine potential perpetrators of electoral conflict, their motives, the potential targets for such conflict, and the tactics utilized in conflict.

At the conclusion of the assessment phase, you will have the information to identify priority areas of electoral security intervention based on the greatest areas of need and possible impact.

ELECTORAL SECURITY PLANNING

The planning phase provides additional filters through which you will continue to refine your priority areas of intervention and your development hypothesis by taking into account:

- **Local change agents** – Which domestic actors have interests aligned with ours, and are they willing to work with us? Do we have access to them? Does the political will exist for programmatic interventions?

- **The international community** – What is the role of the international community in the broader electoral security context?

- **Coordination** – Are there mechanisms in place for coordinating electoral security programs or do they need to be developed?

- **USAID interests and constraints** – What other USG foreign policy priorities and budget issues should be taken into consideration?

At the conclusion of the planning phase, you will have the information to refine priority areas of intervention, update your development hypothesis, develop program objectives, and consider candidate objective-level indicators.

ELECTORAL SECURITY PROGRAMMING

Using your findings from the planning phase, you are now ready to begin programming. While it is not always feasible, the most effective programming strategies usually combine programming activities with both state and non-state stakeholders. By the end of the programming phase, you should have developed a targeted USAID electoral security program that is responsive to the particular needs of any given country context.

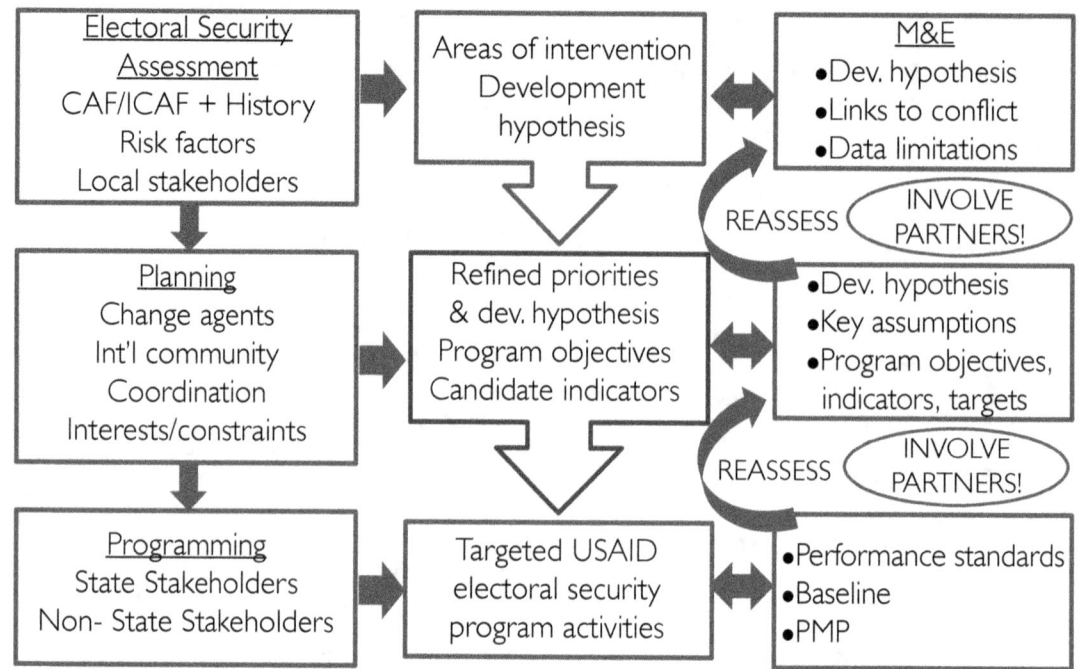

MONITORING AND EVALUATION

Throughout the process, you will be laying the foundation of a strong monitoring and evaluation approach for your electoral security program. During the assessment phase, you will develop an initial problem statement that will lead to your development hypothesis. You will also identify linkages between electoral security issues and broader conflict dynamics. During the planning stage, you will refine

your development hypothesis, articulate key assumptions, and develop program objectives and associated candidate indicators and targets. Finally, during the programming stage, as activities are identified, you will develop performance standards for these activities, identify your baseline, and create a performance management plan. Always remember the importance of involving partners – both domestic and international – in monitoring and evaluation.

INTRODUCTORY TERMS AND DEFINITIONS

A woman casts her ballot at a Rubkona Pakur polling station in South Sudan on April 14, 2010.

This subject matter can be introduced through a trio of fundamental definitions: 1) electoral security; 2) electoral conflict; and 3) electoral justice. Electoral security is the end-state; electoral conflict is the development challenge; and electoral justice is one of the key mitigating factors. These three concepts are discussed in tandem because they collectively embody electoral conflict dynamics.

ELECTORAL SECURITY AND TARGETS

From a broad perspective, four kinds of electoral security (and associated targets) can be identified:

Physical security concerns the protection of facilities and materials, including the electoral commission headquarters and its district offices; registration and polling stations; political party offices; election observer offices; and media organizations. Facilities can also include the residences of election officials or candidates as well as hotels known to be frequented by international visitors, media or observers.

Personal security focuses on electoral stakeholders, including voters, public officials, election workers, security forces, candidates, party agents, election observers and media representatives.[2] The gender, age and ethnicity of human targets should be noted. People can be victims of assassination, torture, sexual

Electoral security can be defined as "…the process of protecting electoral stakeholders such as voters, candidates, poll workers, media, and observers; electoral information such as vote results, registration data, and campaign material; electoral facilities such as polling stations and counting centers; and electoral events such as campaign rallies against death, damage, or disruption."[1]

assault, strategic displacement, physical injury, blackmail or intimidation in attempts to influence their involvement and choices in an election.

Information security concerns protection of computers and communication systems[3] employed in voter registration and vote tabulation, as well as associated sensitive election materials such as voted and un-voted ballots and voter registration lists. Their theft or destruction could have a potential "show stopper" impact on the election.

Electoral events can be victimized by conflict. Events can be official in nature, such as voter registration programs or Election Day activities, but also associated events such as campaign rallies, debates, and political party and coalition meetings.[4] It should be noted that activities such as voter registration are multi-day events and require sustained security over a period of time.

ELECTORAL CONFLICT AND VIOLENCE

While many definitions exist for electoral conflict, some features are consistent. First, electoral conflict has a broad range of manifestations and intensities. The intensity of electoral conflict experienced in the post-election phase of the Popular Consultation in East Timor (1999) and the Kenyan presidential and parliamentary elections (2007) represents the violent end of the spectrum, as thousands of individuals were killed or displaced. By contrast, electoral conflict can manifest itself in acts of personal intimidation as in the case of the Kosovo municipal elections (2000). In this case, the government in Belgrade threatened to discontinue state pensions for Serbs in Kosovo if they participated in those UN-supervised elections.

Second, electoral conflict is employed to achieve political objectives. Capture of the electoral process is done through the elimination of political rivals, suppression of voter turnout, coercion of voters or intimidation of election officials. And, third, electoral conflict and violence can occur during any phase of the electoral cycle. For example, in Bangladesh, political rivals engage in violent attacks on each other during the pre-election phase. In Colombia, the Fuerzas Armadas Revolucionarias de Colombia (FARC), an insurgent guerilla group, employs roadblocks and sabotage on Election Day in an attempt to suppress voter turnout. And, in Zimbabwe (2008), the Zimbabwe National African Party – Patriotic Front (ZANU – PF), the ruling party since independence in 1980, has inflicted retributive violence in the post-election

phase against opposition leaders and supporters of the Movement for Democratic Change (MDC) as well as wavering ZANU – PF voters. These examples demonstrate that electoral conflict can be spontaneous and opportunistic, as in Bangladesh, as well as pre-meditated and centrally directed, as in Zimbabwe.

Therefore, electoral conflict can be defined as "any random or organized act or threat to intimidate, physically harm, blackmail or abuse an electoral stakeholder in seeking to determine, delay or to otherwise influence the electoral process" (Fischer, 2002). It is "at the broadest level, by violence or political violence … the deliberate use of physical harm or the threat of physical harm for a political purpose. Overt physical violence can take the form of beatings, torture, and murder but violence is also evident by its threat – by coercive intimidation. Electoral violence refers to physical violence and coercive intimidation directly tied to an impending electoral contest or to an announced electoral result." (Straus and Taylor 2009)

ELECTORAL JUSTICE

Finally, electoral dispute resolution, or electoral justice, plays a role in electoral security systems. Electoral justice is considered an electoral security concern because fair, expeditious and transparent dispute resolution mechanisms are necessary in order to adjudicate grievances so that the parties are not motivated to go outside of peaceful protocols to press their cases.

Outside of the electoral dispute resolution mandate of courts, election tribunals and Election Management Bodies (EMBs), alternative dispute resolution (ADR) mechanisms can play a role in electoral security. The measures that can be employed range from those conducted by the United Nations (UN) or international figures to those of traditional leaders adjudicating election disputes on the local level. The former is an example of mediation in the violent aftermath of the disputed election in Kenya (2007). The African Union (AU) established the Panel of Eminent African Personalities headed by former UN Secretary General Kofi Annan to lead the negotiations. These efforts resulted in a fragile political agreement, the National Dialogue and Reconciliation. Traditional leaders, such as village chiefs and religious authorities, were engaged in the East Timor Popular Consultation (1999) to successfully adjudicate identity claims for Timorese registering to vote but lacking identification papers or cards.

TABLE 1 ELECTORAL SECURITY TERMS AND DEFINITIONS	
Term	Definition
Delimitation	The process of drawing electoral district boundaries, sometimes referred to as "districting".
Election Management Body (EMB)	The institution legally responsible for managing and overseeing all elements necessary for the conduct of elections – from determining who is eligible to vote to conducting balloting, counting votes, and tabulating results.
Election Management Network	The formal network of public agencies and, in some cases, private sector participants undertaking tasks to assist in the conduct of elections. These may include police, Ministry of Education, local governments, and civil society organizations, among others.
Election Observer	One who witnesses and assesses but does not intervene in electoral proceedings.
Electoral Cycle	Elections as a continuous process rather than an isolated event, often divided into pre-electoral, electoral and post-electoral periods
Electoral Justice	The adjudication of civil challenges to the electoral process filed by voters and political contestants. These civil challenges could concern eligibility, disenfranchisement, campaign practices, irregularities, and other disputed outcomes among others
Electoral Security	Protection of electoral stakeholders (e.g. voters, candidates, poll workers, media and observers); electoral information(e.g. vote results, registration data, and campaign materials); electoral facilities (e.g. polling stations and counting centers); and electoral events (e.g. campaign rallies) against death, damage or disruption
Electoral Security System	The legal architecture, state, and non-state institutions that are employed for the protection of electoral stakeholders and assets; and the adjudicative mechanisms to issue penalties for violations.
Electoral Violence	A sub-type of political violence in which actors employ coercion to advance their interests or achieve specific political ends
Legal Framework for Elections	The broad-ranging legislation and regulations that govern the conduct of electoral stakeholders including: responsibilities of the EMB; behavior of candidates; rules and obligations for the media and political parties; and the use of force by security agents.
Parallel Vote Tabulation	Observers record the results from a scientific sample of polling stations. Results are independently tabulated for comparison with the official results of the election authorities
Transitional Justice	A range of approaches – judicial and non-judicial – that states may use to address past human rights violations. This includes a series of actions or policies and their resulting institutions, which may be enacted at a point of political transition from violence and repression to societal stability.

ELECTORAL SECURITY ASSESSMENT

Voter education poster developed by the Sudanese National Elections Commission and the South Sudan High Committee for distribution during the 2010 elections.

The electoral security assessment is conducted using both a desk study and information gathering in the field. The assessment is composed of three chief areas of analysis.

- **Contextual Analysis:** What are the electoral conflict risk factors found in the security, political, economic, social and public administrative sectors? What other risk factors—such as the type of electoral or political party system—exist?

- **Historical Conflict Factors:** Has there been conflict surrounding past elections?

- **State and Non-state Stakeholders:** What are the characteristics of these stakeholders,

and how do they relate to electoral security? Information gathered through the historical and contextual analysis can be applied to stakeholder analysis to determine potential perpetrators of electoral conflict, their motives, the potential targets for such conflict, and the tactics utilized in conflict.

CONTEXTUAL ANALYSIS

Contextual analysis is conducted on two levels:

First, you will identify the electoral conflict risk factors found in five areas statistically linked to increased likelihood of conflict: the security, political, economic, social and public administrative sectors. This information will ideally build upon a previously conducted CAF or ICAF, which provides a broad contextual overview of the country environment and its relationship with conflict dynamics. It is worthwhile to avoid duplication of data-seeking efforts: existing USG-internal-only resources—such as the CMM Alert List, Political Instability Task Force Lists, and Conflict Early Warning Lists, among others—are statistically-based data models and can be accessed by contacting the DCHA/CMM Office directly.

Second, after identifying the aforementioned five broader sectoral risk factors, you will need to identify election-specific risk factors—such as the type of electoral or political party system—that exist in the country. Rather than being directly data-driven (as above), information for this election-specific context analysis can be gleaned from other desk study materials gathered from host country nationals, local media, assistance implementers, and USAID itself.

SECURITY RISK FACTORS

Elections are target-rich opportunities for insurgencies and rebellions. Voters, candidates, observers, media representatives, election and political party offices and materials could all be attacked by insurgencies in their efforts to disrupt, discredit, or derail an election. Insurgent violence is often countered through a heavy military and police footprint on electoral activities compared with countries where no insurgency is attacking electoral targets. In addition to helping assess patterns of conflict in terms of where it has occurred, the motive, perpetrators and victims of conflict, this information will also be useful for identifying potential "hot spots" that may be especially vulnerable to conflict based on historical precedent or current circumstances (insurgents, criminals). Ongoing insurgencies and rebellions engaged in electoral sabotage can be found in Afghanistan, Iraq, Colombia and the Philippines. The northeastern states of India, Jharkhand and Uttar Pradesh, have also battled a Maoist insurgency attacking electoral targets during state-level elections.

SECURITY FORCES' RULES OF ENGAGEMENT

Security forces that are poorly trained, unequipped, erratically paid or politicized can exacerbate electoral conflict through forceful tactics and incompetence. Rough, even lethal, rules of engagement by police in Zimbabwe (2008) are an example of such tactics. Rules of engagement can also allow riots to continue

and expand. For example, in East Timor (1999) despite a substantial Indonesian security presence, including the army and national police, the local militia was still able to rampage and kill, injure and displace thousands of independence supporters.

POLITICAL RISK FACTORS

REGIME TYPE

The type of regime and the style of governance can influence an election's vulnerability to conflict. Countries in transition to multi-party politics that have been described as "partial, unconsolidated, facade, or gray-zone" democracies may be more vulnerable to electoral conflict given the uncertainties and fragilities of the transition.[5] The influence of the regime type need not be national in character, as there can be localized exposure to electoral violence. Accordingly, elections held in unconsolidated democracies, illustrated as the "Partly Free" category on the Freedom House scale, can be more vulnerable to electoral violence than those countries classified as "Free," or "Not Free." As characterized in USAID country classification descriptions, New and Fragile Democracies as well as Crisis and Rebuilding Societies can be considered at greater risk for electoral violence than Authoritarian or Semi-Authoritarian States.

ECONOMIC RISK FACTORS

A country's economic condition represents another important influence on electoral violence. Poverty and violence are often intimately linked. According to one estimate, by 2010 half of the world's poorest people could be living in states experiencing or at risk of violence.[6] Economic conditions will be evaluated from three perspectives: 1) per capita income; 2) distribution of wealth; and 3) Gross Domestic Product (GDP). These three indicators are noted in literature on electoral violence and have been included accordingly. Some research has suggested that there are economic thresholds that may trigger violence.

PER CAPITA INCOME

One of the economic measures of a nation's wealth is per capita income. According to one set of research, in impoverished countries where the per capita income is less than $2,700 per year, democracy has made the society more conflictive.[7] In the case studies, both Bangladesh and Zimbabwe fail to meet that threshold. Even within a country, less economically developed areas can be more vulnerable to electoral violence than others, as in the Philippines, where the most impoverished provinces in the Autonomous Region of Mindanao are those that have experienced the most electoral violence.[8]

DISTRIBUTION OF WEALTH

Elections represent an economic opportunity to change the distribution of wealth at the national and local levels. When these financial incentives are added to contestants' strategies for winning elections, the likelihood of violence increases.[9] If the distribution of land and resources in society can be measured through income inequality, then the GINI index can be employed as an indicator. The GINI index ranges between 0 to 100 with 0 representing absolute income equality and 100 representing the upper range of income inequality. Scores for Bangladesh, Colombia and Zimbabwe indicate that 50.0 or above may be considered a 'tipping point' for vulnerability. Both Zimbabwe and Colombia have GINI coefficients higher than 50 with Bangladesh approaching that figure.

Bangladesh, Zimbabwe and Colombia provide examples of how land can play a role in electoral conflict. In Bangladesh, the post-election economic shifts described above involve land acquisition pursuits by the winners and land grabs from minorities who are pressured to sell. In Zimbabwe, there has been a recurring pattern of commercial farm invasions escalating in the pre-election period with farmland appropriated for ZANU PF supporters. In addition, the government conducted Operation Murambatsvina ("clear the filth") to break up the urban base of MDC, in 2005. Thousands of homes around Harare were razed and people displaced. This tactic was repeated in 2006 and 2007 against miners through Operation Chikorokoza Chapera ("stop the gold panning"). Post-election violence in 2008 saw further destruction of homes and displacements. In Colombia, land is the territorial control that the spoilers seek to dominate in order to suppress voting, exploit natural resources and protect contraband transit routes.

GDP

With exceptions such as India and the Philippines, electoral conflict has been most common in countries with an annual GDP under $100 billion (USD). Although some research indicates that the relationship is weak, other scholars note that countries in sub-Saharan Africa with lower growth rates have been more vulnerable to electoral conflict than those with higher rates of economic growth.[10] In this research, countries experiencing high levels of electoral violence had an average growth rate in the year preceding the election of 0.83 percent; whereas in countries with no or low electoral violence, the average growth rate was 1.71 percent.

SOCIAL RISK FACTORS

SOCIAL CLEAVAGES

Social cleavages include ethnic, religious, linguistic and regional divides. Social cleavages open vulnerability to conflict through manipulative identity politics. While the post-election violence in Kenya had complex root causes, the face-off was largely tribal in nature with members of President Mwai Kibaki's Kikuyu tribe clashing with opposition leader Raila Odinga's Luos tribe.

DEMOGRAPHIC CHANGES

Major demographic changes in a country can result in conflict. These demographic changes can be immigration, forced displacement or urbanization. The demographic change could be an emerging "youth bulge" and the risks associated with scores of unemployed youth susceptible to recruitment by agents of conflict.

ROLE OF ELITES

Elites may be threatened by an election and either sabotage the process or not recognize the outcomes if disadvantageous to them. For example, in Zimbabwe, the Joint Operation Command (JOC) is a security coordination and command committee involving the military, police, intelligence and penal authorities. There has been a kind of fusion, in effect, between the JOC and ZANU – PF, the ruling party. As a result, speculation is that if ZANU – PF lost an election deemed free and fair by the international community, there is no guarantee that the security elites would recognize such a loss and transfer of power.

DIASPORA ACTIVISM

Migrants and exiles can play a variety of roles in the political life of the homeland bringing a transactional dimension to potential conflict. Mexican politicians campaign in southern California among resident nationals, and several countries including Colombia and Croatia have reserved seats for residents abroad. Diasporas may provide funding for political parties, lobbying on behalf of movements at international organizations, participation in international advocacy networks and supplying recruitment and arms for military movements.[11]

STATE INSTITUTION RISK FACTORS

Are state institutions considered legitimate and effective? Legitimacy refers to the perception by important segments of society that the government is exercising state power in ways that are reasonably fair and in the interests of the nation as a whole. Effectiveness refers to the capability of the government to work with society to assure the provision of order and public goods and services.

ELECTION-SPECIFIC RISK FACTORS

ELECTORAL SYSTEMS AND TYPES

Although a relationship exists between electoral systems and conflict, the risk of electoral system-induced conflict will vary depending upon the political and social context. Accordingly, the advantages and disadvantages of different systems should be evaluated. However, there can be different opinions about which system may reduce violence in any given country context.[12] For example, if a society is experiencing tension rooted in unfair representation of minorities, a majoritarian or "winner-take-all" system might exacerbate that tension, whereas a proportional representation system might alleviate it.

Different types of elections have different conflict dynamics. Presidential elections, for example, are often winner-take-all, high stakes events. In such a scenario, conflict lines may form between factions of the primary contesting parties. In parliamentary elections, the pattern of electoral conflict may be uneven, reflecting sub-national power struggles. Local elections can similarly reflect local political rivalries and capture of local governance can be a high stakes motive. Referenda, by their very nature, create clear winners and losers and often involve high stakes issues such as territorial status.[13]

If electoral stakes are regarded as high value, there may be an incentive to employ violence in their pursuit. For example, in Bangladesh, the winning party gains access to public resources as well as the rents and patronage associated with civil society organizations connected to the party. In 2008, while the pre-election phase produced inter-party violence, the post-election violence was intra-party in nature as the winners competed for resources.

POLITICAL PARTY SYSTEM

Political parties have been termed the "weakest link" in the chain of democratic institution building.

By their competitive nature as vehicles to pursue political power, parties and candidates may intentionally highlight social differences and incite violence as a result of this strategy.[14] Many political parties formed in new and fragile democracies since 1980 were established to compete in an election.

Political party systems can lower incentives for violence through reducing political exclusion, legislating organizational rules, and requiring codes of conduct and internal democracy. Accountability for political finances can dampen the linkages of money and violence. For example, in Bangladesh the term "money and muscle" is used to describe the coercive tactics employed by political parties – vote buying and assault – to influence voting. The prospect of rents and patronage for the winning party fuels intra-party violence in the post-election period. In Zimbabwe, public and natural resources are used to finance the violence. To fund the 2008 post-election violence, the government had only to print more Zimbabwean dollars to pay the perpetrators to act. With the economy now 'dollarized,' the government does not have this funding option, but it reportedly has used diamonds as currency for weapons purchases by the state. And, in Colombia, the guerillas seek drug money, kidnapping ransoms and extortion to fund its operations. The paramilitaries have sought to leverage the wealth that they accumulate for bribes to public officials and vote buying for their candidates. And, illicit funds and violence from traffickers are used to influence local authorities.

QUALITY OF ELECTORAL DISPUTE ADJUDICATION MECHANISMS

The absence of fair, capable and transparent electoral dispute mechanisms can be a risk for potential post-election conflict. If the adjudicative bodies, whether the EMB or the judiciary, are not considered impartial and independent, then grievances that could otherwise be settled by legal means turn conflictive in the pursuit of electoral justice.

DEGREE OF EMB INDEPENDENCE

EMBs not widely viewed as impartial can fatally damage the credibility of the election. The quality and performance of electoral administrators can have a "strong bearing" on whether or not electoral violence occurs.[15] These positive measures include attributes such as inclusive membership structure, political balance and professionalism, which contribute to the legitimacy of the election and, if absent, can trigger election-related violence.[16]

DELIMITATION AND DECENTRALIZATION

The process of delimiting districts can also spark conflict. For example, the headline of an article in the Times of India exclaimed "Was delimitation the trigger?" for violence that broke out between the two castes over reserving a constituency by drawing boundaries favoring one of the castes. The violence reached such intensity that Indian military and paramilitary forces were deployed with "shoot-at-sight" orders to quell the violence.[17] In Sierra Leone, delimitation was listed as a priority policy for the UN Peacebuilding Commission for the Parliamentary elections (2007) and the Local Council Elections (2008). In both cases, Local Council wardens were engaged to prevent conflicts emerging from boundary disputes.[18]

While decentralization initiatives are intended to empower local authorities to be more effective and responsive in rendering public services, an unintended consequence may make the sub-national elections enhanced targets for violence because the electoral stakes of public office have been enhanced.[19]

TIMING AND SEQUENCING OF ELECTIONS

Two kinds of electoral calendars exist: 1) technical calendars and 2) political calendars. Technical calendars govern such activities as ballot printing time, shipping time and asset retrieval time. The political calendar involves such activities as the passage of legislation, appointment of an EMB or reconciliation sufficient to conduct the election. Conflict resolution and elections came together in the first election after the war in Bosnia and Herzegovina (1996). The Dayton Peace Agreement stipulated that the elections were to be held from six to nine months after the accords were signed. However, in many respects, such an electoral calendar re-incentivized sectarian competition and dampened opportunities for short-term reconciliation.

In conflictive environments, the timing of elections must also be considered with respect to the calendar of other associated activities that may impact electoral conflict, including the status of DDR, de-mining measures and the prosecution of war criminals among others. The number of elections that have been held after the so-called "founding" election may be an indicator of increasing democratic consolidation accompanied by diminishing vulnerabilities for electoral conflict.

The sequencing of elections can also result in conflict. For example, the "harmonized" Zimbabwe elections, involving presidential, parliamentary and local voting in the first round, enhanced the electoral stakes and resulted in MDC victories. ZANU – PF forces reacted with retributive post-election violence. However, sequencing can also be employed to manage electoral violence. For example, in India, national elections are conducted on a staggered basis so that security forces can be concentrated in those areas where voting is occurring.

ELECTIONS FOLLOWING REFORMS

While electoral reform can serve to consolidate institutions and processes, it can also create vulnerabilities for electoral conflict. The relationship of real reform and expectation is central to whether such reforms will result in violence. The example of the Solomon Islands is instructive in this regard. An international electoral reform effort was conducted there, raising expectations of a new political dynamic for the islands. However, when the subsequent election returned the incumbent to office, protesters appeared at the parliament building and later set fire to a shopping area.[20] The relationship of real reform and expectation is central to whether such reforms will result in violence. In this regard, "unsubstantial political reforms" may encourage some stakeholders to employ violence as a means of moving forward with their agendas.[21]

ELECTORAL FRAUD OR THE PERCEPTION OF FRAUD

The connection between fraud and violence can be presented as a 'long fuse' where voter confidence in the electoral process is eroded over time and violence is triggered at the announcement of results. It is linked to electoral expectation and the disappointment engendered should those expectations not be met. However, fraud-induced violence can also occur in the pre-election phase. For example, in Mindanao (2009) a hand grenade was thrown at a line of people queuing outside of a local election office registering to vote. There were three people killed and 21 injured. The voters in line were reported to be "flying voters," people who are bused in from another town and paid to register and vote at that location.

ELECTORAL BOYCOTTS

Although participation in a boycott may be difficult to measure, in one study of 50 elections involving boycotts, only 11 of them were reported to be free of violence.[22] Boycotts can commence during the

TABLE 3 ELECTORAL THREATS AND TACTICS BY PHASE	
Election Phase	Threats and Tactics
Phase I: The Long Run-Up to Electoral Events 18 months to 3 months before Election Day	Intimidation or removal of independent judges Intimidation or targeting of election officials Intimidation or harassment of journalists Incitement to violence in the media or public [venue] Police or internal intelligence services targeting of meetings of opposition figures Protecting, expanding, or delineating turf or 'no-go zones' Increased rates of hostage-taking, kidnapping, and extortion
Phase II: The Campaign's Final Lap	Clashes between rival groups of supporters Attacks on election rallies or candidates Bomb scares Attacks or intimidation of election officials Attacks on observers, domestic and international
Phase III: Polling Day	Attacks by armed rebel groups to disrupt the polling, to limit turnout, or to attack security forces on police stations Intimidation of voters to compel them to vote or stay away Attacks on election administrators or observers Physical attacks on election materials such as destruction of ballot boxes
Phase IV: Between Voting and Proclamation	Armed clashes among political parties Violent clashes among groups of rival supporters Vandalism and physical attacks on property of opponents Targeted attacks against specific candidates or political parties
Phase V: Post-Election Outcomes and Their Aftermath	Attacks on rivals who have either won in elections, or were defeated Violent street protests and efforts by armed riot police to maintain or restore order, tear gas, firing on protestors, attacks by protestors on property or the police Emergence of armed resistance groups against an elected government Escalation and perpetuation of ethnic or sectarian violence. [27]

pre-election period or be confined to Election Day. However, the cause and effect relationship can be uncertain. The boycott could be the threat to the elections or a result of threats directed at a candidate, party or group in order to suppress turnout. The National Assembly elections in Thailand (2006) could be cited as an illustrative case of boycotts and violence. The major opposition parties boycotted the election and the ruling Thais Love Thais party of Prime Minister Thaksin Shinawatra won a majority of seats with a very low voter turnout. Street protests took place throughout the electoral cycle. The election was declared undemocratic by the Monarchy and ruled invalid by the Constitutional Court. However, before a new round of elections could be held later that year, a military coup d'état forced the government from power.

POLITICAL CONFRONTATIONS

Political confrontations, when they occur, may lead to violence. Opportunities for such confrontation could be: opponent presence at campaign rallies, campaigning on another party's 'turf' or party agents campaigning at polling stations and counting centers. In Bangladesh, recent reforms aim to minimize opportunities for political confrontation by banning certain kinds of rallies, prohibiting the practice of 'gating' public streets and limiting the number of public address systems at any single rally.

HATE SPEECH AND RUMOR

A free and independent media system is critical for supporting the overall democratic quality of an election. Mis-information and dis-information can be risk factors for electoral conflict. While electronic media can be employed to educate and inform voters, it can also be manipulated as a mass conveyance of incorrect or incendiary information. This practice can occur on state-controlled media or on smaller privately owned but partisan broadcasting companies.

NEW MEDIA

New media including the Internet, SMS messages and social networking sites is an emerging influence in electoral conflict. Due to its reach as an open source of messages and information, new media is flagged here as a risk factor. Web sites can be developed to spread conflictive doctrine to selected audiences; SMS messages can be sent to supporters en masse to call for "flash mobs"; and social networking sites have been used in elections such as the Iranian presidential election (2009) to disseminate video documentation of state-directed violence.

HISTORICAL CONFLICT FACTORS

The country's recent history of electoral conflict should be examined to assess the patterns of violence and ascertain the likelihood that these patterns will recur. The history should identify who and what have been the traditional targets of electoral violence and who have been the perpetrators of that violence. The history should also note the locations, timing and intensity of past violence.[23] The number of years or number of elections since the "founding" election after a conflict or authoritarian rule may be an institutional consolidation vulnerability. That is, risk arguably increases the 'closer' a country is to either of these transition events.

The history of electoral violence might vary from election to election. For example, in East Timor, the 1999 Popular Consultation was beset by pre-election and post-election violence inflicted by local militias loyal to the Indonesian government. By contrast, election violence was diminished in the 2001 Constituent Assembly election and nearly absent from the 2002 presidential election, while the 2007 presidential and parliamentary elections saw a significant increase in electoral violence. By examining the history of conflict for a period of elections the conflict trajectory should be mapped to reveal overall trends.

The country may also have a history of large-scale civil or societal conflict. Early elections conducted after conflicts (and some post-authoritarian scenarios) require special electoral security considerations. For example, the election may take place within the mandate of a UN resolution. Depending on the scope of the mandate, the UN could possess authority over the security and political electoral intervention. Other special considerations that may complicate electoral security in a post-conflict environment include the terms of peace agreements; arms embargoes; damage to infrastructure, Disarmament, De-Mobilization and Re-Integration (DDR) programs; de-mining activities; and the prosecution of war criminals. Without parallel peace-building activities, the post-conflict election may be more vulnerable to conflict.

Within a post-conflict electoral environment, the issue of "demilitarizing politics" is critical to reducing electoral violence. In demilitarizing politics, programming must recognize and support the parallel goals of war termination and democratization. On the one hand, the election organizers must manage security concerns but also create conditions conducive to holding a public event.[24] For example, the failure of the second round of presidential elections to occur in Angola (1992) can be attributed, in part, to the insufficient demilitarization of politics, particularly the Uniao Nacional para a Independencia Total de Angola (UNITA), representing the rebel forces in the election. Although 18 parties contested in the election, the two primary contenders were UNITA and the Movimento Popular de Libertacao de Angola (MPLA), representing the government. Despite some logistical problems, the UN Secretary-General reported that the balloting had been accomplished under relatively peaceful and orderly conditions. However, UNITA claimed widespread fraud in the balloting. The UN sent investigative teams into the field but could not document any claims of systematic or organized fraud. Nevertheless, UNITA pulled out of the election and out of the Joint Political-Military Commission (JPMC), the unified cease-fire enforcement mechanism. The second round of the presidential election was not held and the civil war continued until the assassination of UNITA's leader, Jonas Savimbi, in 2002.

The history of conflict intensity can be evaluated as a possible predictor of future intensities. The ACE Electoral Knowledge Network categorizes the intensity as either a Low Security Risk Environment or a High Security Risk Environment. In Low Security Risk Environments, the employment of the state's security apparatus on a large scale is limited; whereas in a High Security Risk Environment, the EMB must work closely with security forces to prevent, manage or mediate anticipated conflict.[25]

A study of electoral violence in sub-Saharan Africa classified the intensity of conflict on four levels as shown in the table below.

While death and injury represent quantifiable measures of intensity, they are often incomplete because they fail to detect more nuanced forms of intimidation that may have occurred. However, recognizing these limitations, the targets of intimidation can be identified and the numbers affected can be estimated accordingly. Also, if strategic displacement is em-

ployed by spoilers, the numbers of persons displaced should be quantified as a measure of intensity.

STAKEHOLDER ANALYSIS

A combination of state and non-state mechanisms enforce electoral security. A legal architecture legitimizes, empowers and controls these mechanisms. Collectively, these are the components of an electoral security system. Stakeholders can be analyzed in the context of their potential as perpetrators of electoral conflict (and associated motives and tactics utilized) or their potential as targets/victims of such conflict. When determining if stakeholders may be perpetrators of conflict, it is important to determine their motives and whether these motives are longstanding and have been evident in previous elections or if they are recent developments. Then, it must be determined if the means are present for the perpetrator to act, if an opportunity arises. As the table on the adjoining page indicates, different threats emerge during different phases of the electoral calendar. Therefore, profiling must take an electoral cycle approach to map the potential timing of conflict starting as early as 18 months before Election Day. With the targets, perpetrators and tactics noted, the assessment can map the likely conflict chronology through the pre-election, Election Day and post-election phases. In profiling electoral threats, the conflict locations are also variables to define. It is not uncommon for security forces in conflictive electoral environments to designate certain 'hot spots' where conflict is more likely to occur than at other locations. Security assets can be allocated accordingly. In Mexico, the Instituto Federal Electoral (IFE) has developed a State Risk Index to rate the potential for conflict on a state-by-state basis. And, the Election Commission of India (ECI) has developed a Vulnerability Mapping Tool to track incidents for future electoral security planning.

TABLE 2 ELECTORAL INCIDENT CODING	
Code Level	Description
0	No reported electoral violence before or after a vote.
1	The first level of violence is violent harassment, indicated by police breaking up rallies, party supporters fighting, street brawls, opposition newspapers being confiscated, and limited short-term arrests of political opponents.
2	The second level of violence is violent repression, as indicated by long term high-level arrests of party leaders, the consistent use of violent intimidation, limited use of murders and assassinations, and torture.
3	The third level is a highly violent campaign, in which there are repeated, coordinated physical attacks leading to 20 or more deaths[26].

STATE STAKEHOLDERS

State electoral stakeholders can be divided into four institutional categories: 1) regulatory; 2) security; 3) judicial; and 4) public administration.

Three additional state stakeholders that may be indirectly involved with electoral security are intelligence services, penal institutions and human rights commissions. Intelligence services can provide the police with information on pending attacks or profiles on the spoiler leadership. As spoilers are detained for the actions, penal institutions assume the custodial responsibility for their incarceration. And if widespread human rights abuses occur during the election, human rights commissions may launch an investigation or otherwise facilitate a transitional justice intervention.

TABLE 4 STATE STAKEHOLDERS		
Regulatory	Legislature	Responsible to draft electoral and security legislation
	EMBs, media commissions, land and boundary commissions and anti-corruption commissions	Responsible to administer electoral regulations and conduct electoral and related activities according to law and standards
Security Stakeholders	International and national military forces	Responsible to provide an outer security cordon to guarantee a peaceful electoral environment
	International, national and local police; community-based watch committees	Responsible to provide an inner security cordon protecting electoral stakeholders, facilities, materials and events
Judicial Stakeholders	High, Supreme and Constitutional Courts	Responsible for high level electoral judgments such as presidential candidate eligibility or the validity of the certified election results
	International and national electoral dispute resolution	Responsible to adjudicate civil complaints and challenges to the election
	Ordinary Courts	Responsible to adjudicate criminal complaints and award compensation to victims and penalties to perpetrators
	Transitional Justice	Responsible for the prosecution of the perpetrators of electoral conflict in cases of widespread human right abuses
Public Administration Stakeholders	Officials and associated ministries at the national and sub-national levels of government.	Responsible to deliver public services in a nonpartisan and responsive manners to the electorate

NON-STATE STAKEHOLDERS

Non-state enforcement involves stakeholders that employ values-based approaches to monitoring, education, peaceful competition and post-election reconciliation. However, a new category of non-state actors has been identified separately from values-based institutions. Private security companies assist state security institutions in electoral security enforcement.

TABLE 5 NON-STATE STAKEHOLDERS		
CSOs	Election monitoring groups, youth groups, women's organizations, government "watchdogs," and other non-governmental organizations that play a non-partisan role in the election	Responsible to mediate, monitor, and educate on electoral issues
Political Parties	Parties, coalitions and candidacies	Responsible to participate in the election under the laws and regulations of the contest
Media Organizations	Government and private broadcast, print and new media outlets	Responsible to provide accurate and balances news and information about parties, candidates and the electoral process
Traditional Leaders	Community leaders, religious authorities, tribal and clan chiefs	Responsible to provide Alternative Dispute Resolution (ADR) on electoral disputes within their realm of influence and educate their communities about the election
Private Security Companies	Aegis, Armor Group, Edinburgh Risk, GardaWorld, Sabre and others	Responsible to provide contracted security services for election officials, facilities and materials

ELECTORAL SECURITY SYSTEM PROGRAM PLANNING

Polls workers prepare to receive voters at an outdoor polling station in rural Jamjang Mankuo, Sudan on April 11, 2010.

INTRODUCTION TO PLANNING

Electoral security program planning is intended to identify the most appropriate strategies and programs for USAID in a given electoral context. The assessment discussed in the prior chapter yields valuable contextual information including conflict dynamics, resiliencies and mitigating factors, vulnerabilities and opportunities. Building on this information, analysis of key state and non-state actors leads to identification of priority areas of intervention. These areas of intervention are based purely on an electoral security needs assessment for a given country context. The planning process introduces additional variables allowing USAID to further vet

and refine these priority areas by taking into account the identification of local change agents, the presence of international community actors, and USAID's own interests and constraints as a donor.

Although the assessment and planning stages appear as separate sections in the framework document for purposes of clarity, they may overlap depending on the size of the assessment team and the scope of individuals interviewed. Likewise, the order in which the information is presented below does not necessarily represent a sequential approach to planning. In some contexts, for example, it may be most useful to meet first with the country team. In others, these meetings may come at the end so the country team can collectively reflect on how to best complement the activities of other donors.

The important point to remember is that priority areas of intervention should be identified first based on country context. It is important to establish the 'ideal' intervention that can then be further customized and refined based on key international and domestic actors, and donor interests and constraints, rather than beginning with constraints and attempting to craft a responsive program around them.

LOCAL CHANGE AGENTS

The electoral security profile focused on local context. Before factoring in the international community, there is one additional element of the electoral security context that must be considered – change agents. Identifying key local change agents is critical for further refining priority areas of electoral security programming intervention. Successful electoral security programs must establish a clear link between targeted areas of intervention and the ability of local organizations and individuals, many of whom will likely play a key role in implementation, to bring about meaningful change. Three elements should be considered when identifying change agents: 1) political will and access; 2) absorptive capacity; and 3) ability to affect change.

To identify political will, consider the organizations and individuals that have interests consistent with supporting electoral security. This does not necessarily mean that they have the same objectives. Their objectives may be different but the means – electoral security – will be the same. For example, a business association may be interested in supporting electoral security to avoid expensive disruptions to sales. Once organizations and individuals with aligned interests have been identified, ascertain whether or not they are willing to work with USAID. If so, does USAID have access to these organizations and individuals? Access to organizations or individuals may be impeded by the government, poor security conditions, or other considerations that would make programming impractical.

Once political will has been identified, assess the absorptive capacity of these organizations and individuals. It is not uncommon to see a small group of local organizations receive significant resources from multiple donor sources. Are these organizations and individuals in a position to take on additional resources and assume the responsibility of managing multiple programs? The success of USAID's program may depend on the capacity of these organizations

and individuals to receive assistance and implement activities in a manner that is fiscally compliant and meets desired programmatic milestones.

Finally, in the event that political will and absorptive capacity exist, consider the ability of the organization or individual to affect meaningful change. The organization must be credible and able to participate in the political environment in a way that can affect the outcome. Even if they have the technical capacity to implement programs, pouring resources into an organization that lacks credibility in the broader political and social landscape is unlikely to yield the desired results.

Until this point, the assessment and planning phases have focused exclusively on domestic context and actors. Now it is important to overlay the role and priorities of international actors in the electoral security context.

THE INTERNATIONAL COMMUNITY

ROLE OF THE INTERNATIONAL COMMUNITY

Several facets of international community involvement in the electoral context must be explored, including: identifying the role of the international community in elections; ascertaining the possible impact of international community involvement in elections (both intended and unintended); and understanding different international actors' programs, desired outcomes and interests.

It is important to understand the mandate of the international community within the broader electoral context. The mandate defines the characteristics of international involvement and, by extension, the scope and limits of involvement for individual donors. It will also provide a common framework for coordination among international and domestic stakeholders.

Electoral mandates may be included in UN resolutions, terms of peace agreements, or invitations from host countries. Based on the mandate, international actors may play many roles as shown in the table below.[28]

The electoral mandate will influence areas of USAID intervention and have implications for program sustainability and integrating approaches for building local capacity. For example, elections that are supervised and administered by the international

Planning provides an additional 'filter through which USAID can vet and refine priority areas of intervention identified during the electoral security assessment. The planning process will assist with defining:

- Refined priority areas of intervention;

- Updated development hypothesis, program objectives, and candidate indicators at the objective level; and

- A coordination approach for working with other domestic and international stakeholders.

community will require significant local capacity building in anticipation of future elections, versus elections
managed and administered by the host country with
international support.

Given the diverse nature of international involvement in elections, it is also important to be aware
of the potential impact, intended and unintended, of
international involvement and the ramifications on
potential USAID programs (see International Community Involvement text box).

PROFILE OF THE INTERNATIONAL COMMUNITY

In addition to understanding the broad mandate of
the international community in the elections context,
the international actors themselves must be taken
into account. The sheer number as well as diverse

interests and capacities of these organizations can
present a challenge to integrated elections planning.
Accordingly, understanding the relationship among
international community programs and the electoral
context is critical for refining USAID's programming
priorities to avoid duplication and to better understand the limitations of the environment.

Several types of international actors that play a role
in electoral security programming include:

• USAID;

• Other US Government Agencies;

• UN;

• Regional Inter-governmental Organizations;

• Other Governments;

TABLE 6 ELECTORAL INTERVENTION MODELS FOR ELECTION SECURITY PROGRAMMING		
Intervention	Examples	Description
Electoral Supervision	Namibia and Bosnia and Herzegovina	Through a UN resolution or peace agreement, the international community is requested to supervise an election or referendum
Electoral Administration	Cambodia, East Timor, Kosovo	Through a UN resolution or peace agreement, the international community is requested to administer an election or referendum
Electoral Verification	Nicaragua, Angola, El Salvador	Through a UN resolution or peace agreement, the international community is requested to verify an election or referendum
Electoral Certification	East Timor, Côte d'Ivoire	Through a UN resolution, peace agreement, or invitation by host country, the UN evaluates each stage of the electoral process and assesses its compliance to international good practices
Electoral Assistance	New democracies	Through an invitation from a domestic electoral stakeholder, the international community can be requested to assist sovereign domestic institutions with the conduct of an election or referendum or the adjudication of the results
Electoral Monitoring	New democracies	The purposeful gathering of information about an electoral process and public assessment of that process against universal standards for democratic elections by responsible foreign or international organizations committed to neutrality and to the democratic process for the purpose of building public and international confidence about the election's integrity or documenting and exposing the ways in which the process falls short.[29]
Electoral Mediation	Nicaragua, Kenya	A form of electoral engagement whereby an impartial third party employs non-official election dispute resolution mechanisms with the objective to obtain acceptable electoral results from all domestic stakeholders

- International Non-Governmental Organizations;

- Others.

Actors from USAID Washington and the field whose activities may intersect with electoral security program planning include:

- Field Mission Directors;

- Regional bureaus;

- Democracy, Conflict and Humanitarian Assistance (DCHA)/DG – Office of Democracy and Governance;

- DCHA/CMM – Office of Conflict Management and Mitigation;

- DCHA/OTI – Office of Transition Initiatives;

- DCHA/OMA – Office of Military Affairs;

- DCHA/OCR – Office of Civilian Response – Civilian Response Corp – Active or Standby.

In addition, DCHA/OFDA – Office of Foreign Disaster Assistance and DCHA/FFP – Office of Food for Peace may also be engaged if, for example, elections correspond with a natural disaster or there is a humanitarian crisis yielding large numbers of internally displaced persons.

Other US Government Agencies, such as Department of State, Department of Justice, and Department of Defense will likely play a role in electoral security.

Department of State (DoS): The Embassy will provide in-country policy guidance. Regional bureaus will provide support to Embassies and are also responsible for overall policy development. The Political and Military Affairs Bureau may be involved in DDR programs and security sector reform (SSR) as related to peacekeeping operations. The International Organizations Bureau coordinates US contributions to peacekeeping missions, and the Population, Refugees, and Migration Bureau works on issues of refugee reintegration. Other DoS actors may include the Democracy, Human Rights and Labor Bureau; Office of the Coordinator for Reconstruction and Stabilization, Public Diplomacy, and the International Narcotics and Law Enforcement Bureau.

Department of Justice (DoJ): The International Criminal Investigative Training Assistance Program works with host country police and foreign governments to develop professional, transparent law enforcement institutions. Overseas Prosecutorial Development Assistance and Training works with host country prosecutors and judicial personnel to develop and sustain effective criminal justice institutions.

Department of Defense (DoD): The DoD presence will vary depending on whether or not there is a U.S. military presence in-country, such as in Iraq or Afghanistan. Within USAID, the Office of Military Affairs serves as a liaison between USAID and DoD. Actors that may have a role in electoral security programs may include: the Defense Liaison Officer at the Embassy, Combatant Commands (COCOMs) and Provincial Reconstruction Teams (PRTs).

Both the National Security Council (NSC) and the US Congress can have a significant impact on policy and resource allocation. Chaired by the President, the NSC is the highest level political and policy entity and the President's principal forum for considering national security and foreign policy matters and consists of his senior national security advisors and cabinet officials. The US Congress can authorize or block electoral assistance to a particular country. By shifting priorities, Congress has the power to restructure allocations in order to impede or facilitate electoral assistance.[30] The role of the intelligence community in collecting and analyzing data on potential conflict should also be noted.

UNITED NATIONS AND OTHER INTER-GOVERNMENTAL ORGANIZATIONS

The UN has played an instrumental role in electoral security since 1989. In the last several years, the UN has moved toward more integrated missions that directly link security and conflict management, human rights, humanitarian, development and democratization efforts into a common country-level plan.[31] It is common to find the following entities of the UN in the context of elections:

- UN Electoral Assistance Division (UNEAD) – serves as the focal point for electoral policy and coordination of UN actors;

- UN Department of Peace Keeping Operations (UN DPKO) – includes both international military and civilian police to provide election security and overall mission management;

- UN Development Program (UNDP) – provides project funding and may manage multi-country trust funds;

Regional Inter-Governmental Organizations often play a constructive role by providing a set of professional standards and common principles for conducting elections. They may also provide international observers. These organizations include:

- African Union (AU)

- Organization of American States (OAS)

- European Union (EU)

- Organization for Security and Cooperation in Europe (OSCE)

- Southern Africa Development Community (SADC)

- Council of Europe

- League of Arab States

- Organization of the Islamic Conference (OIC)

- Commonwealth of Independent States (CIS)

- La Francophonie

- The Commonwealth

- UN Volunteers (UNV) – provides international elections officers at registration sites and polling stations;

- UN Office for Project Services (UNOPS) – provides logistical support.

In addition to the UN, regional Inter-Governmental Organizations (IGOs) may play a role in electoral security. Many of these organizations provide a set of professional standards and common principles for what constitutes free and fair elections (see Regional Inter-governmental Organizations text box). They may also address key conflict prevention issues through electoral observation missions. For examples of regional standards, see "Compendium of International Standards for Elections" at – http://ec.europa.eu/europeaid/what/human-rights/election_observation_missions/index_en.htm

GOVERNMENTS, NON-GOVERNMENTAL ORGANIZATIONS (NGOS) AND OTHERS

In addition to the US, other governments also provide funding and technical expertise in support of electoral security programs. The government may implement programs or do so through NGOs. In the context of electoral security programming, some of the most active governments include: Australia, Canada, Denmark, Finland, Germany, the Netherlands, Norway, Sweden, Switzerland, the United Kingdom, Mexico, Brazil, India and Japan.

NGOs may implement government- funded programs. Some of the more prominent NGOs providing election-related assistance include:

- International Foundation for Election Systems (IFES) based in the US;

- Electoral Institute of Southern Africa (EISA) based in South Africa;

- Electoral Reform International Services (ERIS) based in the UK;

- Bureau for Institutional Reform and Democracy (BIRD) based in Germany.

Other electoral security actors may include the International Institute for Democracy and Electoral Assistance (IDEA) and Election Management Associations (EMAs). IDEA represents 25 member states focused on enhancing electoral knowledge and elections administration globally. IDEA may provide information about electoral security and best practices. EMAs

provide assistance and observers. Their efforts may be national, regional or international in scope.[32]

COORDINATION

When assessing the different international actors and their respective contributions to electoral security programming, it is important to consider how different stakeholder activities are, or are not, coordinated. Depending on the coordinating mechanisms already in place, there may be a convening or leadership role for USAID.[33]

Coordination of Key International Community Actors: The UN often acts as the lead coordinating body for the international community, but USAID can play a key leadership and coordinating role either bilaterally or as a member of a UN-led core group. In other cases, the overall coordination function may not be present. Coordination among international actors is critical for ensuring unity of message and avoiding duplication of financial and technical assistance. In addition to routine working-level coordination, it is important to have a high-level diplomatic committee to ensure that policy issues are discussed and decisions made. These committees may also play a critical role in mediating disputes and brokering compromises among political factions.

Coordination with the Military and Police: Close coordination with a US-led coalition, international peacekeepers, and national military and police forces, as feasible, is critical for mapping a country's electoral risk profile and strategically allocating security assets. It is also important to ensure coordination with civilian actors, such as elections observers, and to clarify the mission and rules of engagement of both military and police in the broader electoral context.

Coordination within the US Government: Coordination within the US Government will likely involve the Embassy Political Section, USAID Democracy Office, DoS Public Diplomacy Office and the Military Liaison Officer. A similar group should be formed in Washington, DC. Both groups, field and Washington, should meet regularly to coordinate and share information on strategy, activities, responsibilities, timelines and changing circumstances.

Coordination with Local Actors: In many countries, USAID will already have established relationships with local actors engaged in different aspects of the electoral cycle. Where USAID does not have such relationships, electoral security assessments should be employed to help identify and profile key electoral security stakeholders. These local actors should be brought into the planning process to ensure that proposed activities are relevant and meaningful within the country context. Engaging local actors in the planning process may also serve as a capacity building activity for some organizations. Where feasible, national military and police forces may also have a role to play in the context of coordinated electoral security programming.

USAID INTERESTS AND CONSTRAINTS

Finally, USAID's interests and constraints as a donor should be considered when refining priority areas of intervention. USAID interests will include considerations of broader US Government foreign policy. Elections are often high profile events that capture the attention of policy makers, and the Embassy may play a significant role in program design and implementation. Additionally, consider the comparative advantages and where USAID can make a significant contribution in light of other existing or planned electoral security programs. Other issues include opportunities to leverage existing USAID, US Government or other donor programs, such as an on-going civil society strengthening program or judicial reform initiatives, that may advance the electoral security programs under consideration,

As stated previously, high profile and politically charged activities like electoral security often receive heightened scrutiny from US Government policy makers, US citizens, and the international community. Increased scrutiny may lead to pressure to demonstrate rapid and tangible results, which may also have implications for program planning. In this context, if USAID determines that planned interventions will require an extended period of time to demonstrate results, consideration might be given to including some activities that will yield more immediate outputs or outcomes.

Legal, budgetary, and human resource constraints may also affect programming considerations. Restrictions on foreign aid or sanctions may be in place against certain countries for violations of loan repayment requirements, human rights conventions, nuclear non-proliferation pacts or acts of war. While this does not necessarily preclude assistance, it may require seeking special approvals or waivers.[34]

Budget considerations, both the amount and source of available funding, may also have implications for program planning. For example, while Development Assistance (DA) often comes from USAID, Economic Support Funds (ESF) come from Department of State, which might want some involvement in how

the money is spent.[35] In cases where there are urgent and unexpected Election and Political Processes (EPP) needs that a Mission's current operating year budget (OYB) cannot sufficiently address, the DCHA/DG Office manages a special EPP Fund.

Finally, it is important to take Mission capacity into consideration. Does the mission have adequate staffing to assume responsibility for the program being designed? If the program will require substantial amounts of management and Mission staff is already stretched, alternative activities may need to be considered.

Analysis of the planning variables described above will provide the additional information required to:

- Reprioritize areas for USAID electoral security interventions;

- Refine development hypotheses;

- Develop program objectives linked to the priority areas of intervention and candidate indicators at the objective level;

- Design a coordinated approach consistent with coordination needs and opportunities at different levels.

The Elections and Political Process (EPP) Fund meets urgent or unanticipated needs such as snap elections, coups, transitional justice, power sharing arrangements or post-elections violence. Funds are awarded using a competitive process in which applications are required to meet at least two of the following three criteria : the proposed program 1) is unique and innovative, 2) addresses snap elections or other unanticipated needs, and 3) has the ability to have a significant and measurable impact.

Negotiating Constraints - In one African country, the Ambassador wanted international election observers – a high profile activity with immediate results, but very costly. Upon conducting an electoral security assessment, the team concluded that improving electoral security was contingent on strengthening the role of civil society organizations (CSOs) in elections – a much longer-term type of intervention. The team knew that bringing in international observers would take most of the program budget, leaving little else for other activities. So, they proposed a compromise. The team suggested using regional observers from the Electoral Institute of Southern Africa (EISA). This solution ensured quick results, while also strengthening regional capacity to conduct electoral observation missions. Additionally, there were sufficient funds remaining to focus on strengthening the capacity of CSOs to play a meaningful role in longer-term, sustainable election security.

ELECTORAL SECURITY SYSTEM PROGRAMMING

Poll workers sort ballot materials in advance of the July 2009 presidential elections in Indonesia.

Electoral security programming is intended to develop legal architectures guiding state and non-state stakeholders in the capacity to prevent, manage or mediate electoral conflict. Such programming involves both rules-based and values-based approaches to ensure peaceful electoral competition and post-election reconciliation.

STATE ELECTORAL SECURITY STAKEHOLDERS

REGULATORY STAKEHOLDERS

LEGISLATIVE ASSISTANCE

If the legal architecture for electoral security requires reform, then constitutional, legislative and regulatory programming can be provided to assist these reforms. Election crimes, penalties, enforcement authority and use of force regulations are election security elements that must be present in the overall electoral legal architecture. Technical assistance can be provided to legislative drafting committees to develop language for the reform measures.

EMB INTEGRITY BUILDING PROGRAMS

If the partiality or performance of an EMB is generating conflict, then electoral interventions to build the integrity and capacity of the EMB can take a number of forms. Conventional capacity building and assistance programs for EMBs and other regulatory stakeholders can be leveraged to prevent electoral conflict by "generating legitimacy," as the UNDP terms it, through capable and transparent administration. Integrity building activities include EMB membership in regional associations of election officials, transparency in meetings and decisions, broadly representative pools of poll workers, and employing new media for communications and complaint resolution among other programs.

TARGETED "DE-CONFLICTIVE" ELECTORAL ASSISTANCE

If there are particular points of contention in the performance of an EMB, then targeted assistance programs can address those particular activities causing conflict. UNDP's involvement in Bangladesh is an example of using special technical assistance to target a potential trigger for conflict. The parliamentary elections in 1996 and 2001 were marred by violence. The actions of the Bangladesh Election Commission (BEC) were regarded as politicized. Many of the political tensions going back to 1996 concerned the voter registry. In order to reduce tensions surrounding the voter registry, UNDP implemented the Preparation of Electoral Roll with Photographs project in 2007 with parliamentary elections occurring in December 2008. While the voter registry was only one contentious issue, the UNDP intervention diminished the likelihood that voter registry manipulation would become a trigger for electoral violence.[36]

ELECTORAL SECURITY ADMINISTRATION

If the EMB lacks specialized capacity in electoral security administration, then programming can be directed at building that capacity through organizational development and informational resources. EMBs should have the capacity to develop an electoral security concept and plan. Assistance can be provided to the EMB to establish coordination mechanisms such as joint electoral security task forces involving the military. If international security forces are present, the task force should include their representatives as well. Another feature of election security administration is decentralization. Such decentralization is necessary because the nature and intensity of the threat will vary from locale to locale. Therefore, the assistance programming may require a sub-national component for coordination to be effective on the local level.

The Figure below illustrates the coordination dynamic in electoral security administration.

For informational resources, collecting and mapping data on electoral incidents is another electoral security administration program for EMBs. Software can be developed to establish an Electoral Incidents Database that tracks and profiles electoral conflicts. However, such a database will only have value to the extent that the information collected is accurate and consistent in reporting format. One example of such a reporting framework used to monitor electoral violence can be found in the USAID-funded Electoral Violence Education and Resolution (EVER) Program at IFES. The EVER Program is an electoral monitor-

FIGURE 2: ELECTORAL SECURITY ADMINISTRATION COORDINATION

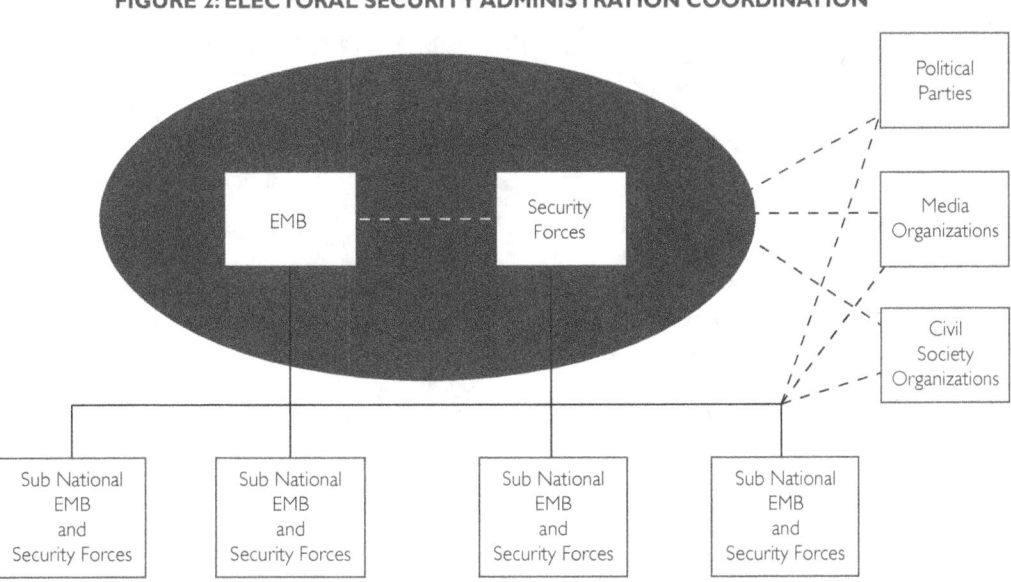

ing program that focuses on electoral conflict and violence. The EVER reporting format collects six types of data: 1) Location of Violence; 2) Source of Information; 3) Type of Violence; 4) Victim of Violence; 5) Perpetrator of Violence; and 6) Consequences of Violence.

The Centre for Monitoring Electoral Violence (CMEV), a unit of the Centre for Policy Alternatives in Sri Lanka, employs a similar methodology, as described on its web site: "CMEV records incidents of murder, attempted murder, assault, abduction, arson, robbery, grievous hurt and threats and intimidation as 'major incidents', while damage to property, threats, mischief and violations of election law are recorded as 'minor' incidents."

Another method of electoral security data collection was employed in Afghanistan in 2005 by distributing a District Security Questionnaire for the Joint Election Management Body Secretariat's (JEMBS) Security Department. The form included 38 questions that concerned the demographics of the location, security situation, threats and warnings, security support and logistics. Based upon an evaluation of the responses from election and security officials, each of the 72 districts at the time received a "Threat State" of Permissive, Semi-Permissive, or Non-Permissive.

SECURITY STAKEHOLDERS

If security organizations, particularly the national and local police, require electoral security assistance, it can be provided in the form of training programs, specialized enforcement capacity, and standards for the rules of engagement. While the focus of this programming is on the police, national militaries can play a role in electoral security. In Bangladesh, 50,000 troops were deployed around election time and the army played a key logistical role in the conduct of voter registration. The army plays a similar security role in Colombia; more than 100,000 troops and police are deployed on Election Day to protect polling stations.

CIVIL-MILITARY RELATIONS PROGRAMS

The USAID technical publication Civil-Military Relations: USAID's Role identifies various illustrative programs that can be undertaken in civil-military relations. However, working in an electoral context poses special constraints on civil-military programming. First, if the military plays a role in the conduct of the elections, an assessment should be made about whether this role promotes democratic consolidation or subverts it. Second, the military should

be under civilian control or reforming in that direction. And third, an assessment should be made about the ability and willingness of the military to accept programming. While the militaries in Bangladesh and Colombia have played positive and effective roles in electoral security and logistical assistance to the EMB, Zimbabwe represents the other end of the spectrum where the military was a culprit in post-election conflict.

POLICE ELECTION TRAINING PROGRAMS

Below is an example of the core curriculum for a police and electoral security training program that could be used to train police in electoral security practices:

- The nature of the electoral legislation and an overview of the electoral process;

- The role of the police in supporting the democratic process;

- Human rights issues in relation to the police's role in the election;

- Security objectives and strategy in relation to the election;

- The standards of professional, neutral and non-intimidating conduct to be upheld by police forces during the election;

- Contact mechanisms and liaison details (on an as needed basis) between the electoral commission and police forces;

- Details of specific offenses against electoral laws;

- Details of other laws such as those regarding public gatherings that will have an impact on police planning.[37]

One example of such a training program is the International Criminal Investigation Training Assistance Program (ICITAP) run by the US Department of Justice. ICITAP conducted an election training program for police in Macedonia (2002) through the Public Defense Unit in coordination with the Ministry of Interior and funded by the Open Society Institute of Macedonia and the Constitutional and Legal Policy Institute. It was a one-day Election Security Training Course for 3,500 uniformed and reserve officers. The training was conducted over 54 sessions by six mobile training teams in 15 different locations.

JOINT ELECTION OPERATIONS CENTERS

The establishment of Joint Election Operation Centers (JEOCs) during electoral cycles provides a physical location for the coordination and communication of electoral security enforcement. At the JEOC, security forces and election officials coordinate planning, share information and track electoral incidents. The ACE Electoral Knowledge Network suggests an expanded list of potential participants in JEOC activities to include senior election managers; security forces, civil emergency and rescue services; political party agents; civil society organizations monitoring the election; conflict resolution specialists; women's groups and traditional leaders.

JUDICIAL STAKEHOLDERS

ELECTORAL DISPUTE RESOLUTION MECHANISMS

If the mechanisms for electoral dispute resolution are weak or ineffective, then assistance can be directed to develop the capacity of these institutions. Just as EMBs must be impartial and possess sufficient capacity to conduct the election, judicial institutions must be similarly equipped to fairly and transparently adjudicate disputes so that these grievances do not turn violent. The ACE Electoral Knowledge Network classifies election dispute systems as conducted by the judiciary, EMBs, or specially appointed election tribunals, among other bodies. The table below shows a global survey of such models.

Although each model possesses strengths and weaknesses, the de-conflictive elements are more an issue of the characteristics of justice – fair, responsive, and transparent – and the independence of the adjudicator from the government and other political interests. Capacity building programs that better enable dispute adjudicators to perform that work can take the form of assistance with operational planning for processing disputes, voter education programs about

dispute mechanisms, decentralization of adjudication and 'triaging' procedures for complaint management, and exchanges with other election dispute management bodies.

In some post-conflict electoral environments, the international community has established ad hoc election dispute resolution mechanisms that supervise the complaints process. Examples include Bosnia and Herzegovina (1996), the Electoral Appeals Sub-Commission (EASC) in Kosovo (2000) and the Electoral Complaints Commission (ECC) in Afghanistan (2005 – 2009). In each case, the judicial panel was composed of both international and domestic jurists. The OSCE organized the initiatives in the Balkans while the UN led those in Afghanistan. For the first round of the presidential election in Afghanistan (2009), the ECC played a pivotal role in investigating and adjudicating fraud, sending the vote to a second round.

DOMESTIC COURTS

If domestic courts are legitimate venues for justice, then domestic judicial remedies can be employed to rectify the impact of violence on an election. For example, in Nigeria, the ordinary courts overturned an election that was deemed to be too violent and fraudulent. The Court of Appeals in Ibadan, Nigeria, nullified the results of a senatorial election (2009) because it was marred by "violence, thuggery, and intimidation."[39] Domestic courts can also play a role in redressing the grievances of the victims of electoral violence. This redressing not only includes the prosecution of the perpetrators, but also the consideration of reparations for untimely death, disabling injury or property destruction.[40]

TRANSITIONAL JUSTICE MECHANISMS

If the level of electoral violence has caused widespread human rights abuses, then some form of transitional justice can be considered. For the first time, the International Criminal Court (ICC) is in-

TABLE 7 ELECTORAL DISPUTE RESOLUTION MECHANISMS		
Institution	Number of Countries	Percent of Countries
Judiciary	103	51.7%
EMB	89	44.7%
Specially Appointed Electoral Tribunal	30	15.0%
Other	24	12.0%
No Information available	5	2.5%
Not Applicable	1	0.5%[38]

volved in an electoral conflict case, the post-election violence in Kenya (2007 and 2008). The entrance of the ICC was prompted by the failure of the government to establish a special tribunal to adjudicate the alleged crimes. In cases such as Kenya, the level of violence was sufficient to trigger some transitional justice interventions. According to the International Center for Transitional Justice, widespread violations of human rights call for transitional justice responses. Transitional justice recognizes the victims yet seeks to promote peace and reconciliation. Transitional justice can employ a number of mechanisms including criminal prosecutions, truth commissions, reparations programs, gender justice, security sector reforms and memorialization efforts.[41]

NON-STATE ELECTORAL SECURITY STAKEHOLDERS

Non-state electoral security activities involve stakeholders in values-based approaches to peaceful competition and post-election reconciliation. The principal stakeholders include civil society organizations, political parties, media organizations and traditional leaders.

The list below summarizes program concepts of non-state electoral security mechanisms cited by UNDP:

- Multi-stakeholder forums and consultations in preparation for a public campaign;

- Electoral assistance groups whose members serve as volunteer poll workers or monitors;

- Peace campaigns through civil society organizations;

- Religious and cultural leaders' forums;

- Traditional leaders' forums;

- Strategic leadership development and training.[42]

In addition, international election monitoring initiatives have been shown to have a dampening effect on electoral conflict in some cases. Having international "witnesses" to criminal acts can discourage the potential perpetrators from acting. In addition, the Declaration of Principles for International Election Observation states, "the findings of international election observation missions provide a factual common point of reference for all persons interested in the elections, including the political competitors. This can be particularly valuable in the context of disputed elections, where impartial and accurate findings can help to mitigate the potential for conflicts."

CIVIL SOCIETY ORGANIZATION PROGRAMS

Civil society organizations (CSOs) are principally involved through roles in mediation, monitoring and education. The role of new media is also examined in this section. While the monitoring program described below directly concerns electoral conflict, conventional international and domestic observation programs can also assume a "conflict lens" and take note of incidents observed or reported. For example, Parallel Vote Tabulation (PVT) can serve as an instrument to validate the election outcomes in disputed contests.

ELECTORAL MEDIATION

If disputing electoral stakeholders agree to discuss their disagreements, electoral mediation can be employed as a form of electoral engagement whereby an impartial third party provides non-official electoral dispute resolution services. Electoral mediation can be preventative in nature, provide on-going conflict management or serve as an instrument for crisis responses. It is an Alternative Dispute Resolution mechanism and a non-state enforcement reflection of electoral justice.

For example, under funding from the Division for Human Security of the Swiss Foreign Ministry, an NGO-based electoral conflict prevention program was organized for the 2004 presidential and parliamentary elections in Mozambique. Under this program, a network of local NGOs performed monitoring in general but also helped to change the content of the campaign rhetoric. The local network brought together major religious groups and other organizations with good reputations to change the debate in support of peace. The network also changed the character of debates among candidates, forcing them to focus on the issues and political content versus personalities. There was no reported conflict after the 2004 elections.[43]

ELECTORAL CONFLICT MONITORING

If electoral incidents are common and widespread, then programming should be directed at profiling the threat, monitoring incidents and documenting for later redress.

IFES and CMEV conduct electoral monitoring that is focused on incident reporting and profiling. Their program methodologies were described in an earlier section. However, speaking to its EVER experience in the Kyrgyz election (2005), IFES reports the following lessons learned:

- The timeliness, quality and efficiency of the reports on election-violence incidents were critical and under constant scrutiny as the information was used directly in intervention efforts to prevent further violence;

- The publication of weekly bulletins provided objective, informative evaluation of the nature, extent and locality of problems and efforts to manage election-related conflicts; and

- The training and collaborative work with local NGOs allowed for the efficient development and transfer of capacity to Kyrgyzstani organizations.[44]

ELECTORAL DISPUTES MONITORING

If electoral justice mechanisms are opaque and result in conflict, then election dispute monitoring can be conducted as well. For example, the OSCE has developed an Election Dispute Monitoring System, in keeping with the election cycle approach to election security, which divides the electoral calendar as follows: pre-election registration; election campaign; Election Day issues; post voting issues and general issues.[45]

Just as electoral incidents can be entered onto a database for reference and tracking, a Database for Election Disputes can be developed. The OSCE database codes cases according to the following criteria: Number, Court/Election Commission/Other Institution, Date, Region, Constituency, Complaints, Accused, Summary, Status, Comments, Legal Basis of Complaint, Decision, Enforcement, and Category.[46] With this data the patterns of complaints can be tracked. The OSCE Handbook can be found at:

http://www.osce.org/publications/odi-hr/2000/08/12350_130_en.pdf.

EDUCATION PROGRAMS

Civil society organizations can also engage in peace and civic education programs. Guinea-Bissau experienced electoral conflict in the early 2000's. Taking steps to prevent violence in the ramp-up to 2005 elections, the International Peace Project formed a new group – the Citizens' Goodwill Task Force (CGTF) – to conduct a national campaign in voter education and peacebuilding. The CGTF's activities included media events and candidate debates. On Election Day, the CGTF deployed "peace brigades" at polling stations who assisted poll workers and mediated minor disputes among voters. The election was largely incident free.[47]

Diasporas can also be encouraged to provide an educational function. For example, Armenians in the UN support newspapers in Armenia, newsletters, Internet sites and e-mail distribution lists, all of which can be engaged in positive electoral activism.

NEW MEDIA

New media can be employed for rapid dissemination of messages (SMS and social networking sites), documentation of electoral conflict (mobile phone videos) and information resources (Internet). The use of SMS messaging, Facebook, Twitter, Livejournal blogs and mobile telephone videos by the Green Movement in Iran after the disputed presidential election (2009) has been previously noted. Web sites not only convey information, but can be employed as tools to support protests, demonstrations and "flash mobs."

New media can also be employed in electoral monitoring. In Russian local elections (2010), video footage was put on YouTube of a polling station chairman in the city of Azov as he attempted to mix fraudulent ballots pre-marked for the United Russia Party into the ballot box with the other legitimate ballots. SMS as a tool for election observation reporting is said to have started in Indonesia (2005), where domestic observers first used SMS to receive reports from 750 election monitors in the field. And, in the Palestinian Legislative Council election (2006), NDI employed SMS messaging to coordinate the activities of international observers. The Montenegrin independence referendum (2006) was the first time that SMS was employed to systematically gather results and turnout data in order to perform outcome projections.[48]

POLITICAL PARTY PROGRAMS

Two common instruments to engage political parties in prevention, management and mediation of electoral conflict are the use of political party councils and the adoption of codes of conduct.

POLITICAL PARTY COUNCILS

If communication among political parties and between political parties and state enforcement institutions is poor, then programming can be directed at establishing communication mechanisms. For example, in the Sierra Leone presidential and parliamentary elections (2007), UNDP, through the United Nations Observation Mission in Sierra Leone (UN-OMSIL), provided support for the creation of the Political Parties' Registration Commission (PPRC), a program to strengthen parties as well as to anticipate and mediate disputes and prevent conflict. The PPRC engaged in an inter-party discussion and developed a code of conduct to guide party members' conduct.

POLITICAL PARTY CODES OF CONDUCT

If there is a need to reform and de-conflict political party behaviors, then the adoption of political party codes of conduct can be considered. The codes mandate specific conduct and behaviors that define both prohibitions and positive actions. Prohibitions include hate speech, defacing campaign posters, disrupting campaign events and intimidating voters. Positive actions include encouraging women to be candidates and party leaders. Codes may also encourage the involvement of youth in the party activities. Some codes describe prohibitions on certain financial receipts and expenditures of political parties. However, without legally binding political finance enforcement capacity, the code alone can be a weak instrument for financial regulation.

To strengthen the code enforcement, the terms of the codes of conduct can be mandated in legislation. For example, in Malawi the Parliamentary and Presidential Elections Act tasked the Electoral Commission with the establishment and enforcement of a political party code. The terms of the code of conduct are legally binding and can be enforced with legal sanctions. South Africa is another such example where the political party code is derived from the Electoral Act and promulgated and enforced by the Independent Electoral Commission.

MEDIA ORGANIZATION PROGRAMS

MEDIA CODES OF CONDUCT

Media organizations can be a source of voter education and public information; however, media can also serve as the conveyor of hate speech, incendiary rumors and dangerous falsehoods. For example, the Guyana Broadcasting Corporation was accused of inciting violence by airing false reports about voters being turned away at polling stations and provoking and attacking the headquarters of the Guyana Elections Commission in 1992.

Specific to elections, the ACE Electoral Knowledge Network has developed a model Code of Conduct for Election Reporting that cites 20 indicators of professional responsibility as behavioral standards. Some of the indicators concern expectations of objectivity, truth, responsiveness to the needs of voters, provi-

sion of relevant information, encouraging free speech, and promoting democratic values. The model Code also cites prohibitions such as hate speech and incitement, refraining from publishing in some circumstances, not accepting gifts, not favoring the incumbents, and refraining from biased reporting on women. The Code cites other obligations to investigate stories, provide equitable coverage of political parties, offer a forum for alternative views and assist the EMB with official electoral message dissemination. Finally, the Code puts forward certain obligations to media owners, whether the state or private interests. The Code suggests that electoral issues be given priority space or air time over other issues while the electoral campaign is being conducted.

In response to the abuses of the past as described above, the Guyana Press Association announced its commitment to develop a media code of conduct in 2006. This initiative was supported by UNDP. Another example of a media code of conduct specific to elections can be seen in 2007 in Sierra Leone. The adoption process was a collaborative effort of the Sierra Leone Association of Journalists, the National Electoral Commission, the Political Parties Registration Commission and civil society organizations. The initiative was facilitated by the UN.

MEDIA MONITORING

If there is a media code of conduct, then monitoring compliance with its terms is a potential program activity. At the same time, media monitoring can include tracking media reports for mis-information, dis-information and rumor so that remedial responses can be quickly formulated and disseminated. The monitoring can be performed by the EMB as in the case of Guyana, or by domestic and international observer groups. In Guyana, the Elections Commission established the Media Monitoring Unit (MMU) to analyze the content of broadcast news for accuracy and impartiality. The MMU published regular reports on their findings. Unlike previous elections, there were no incidents reported to have been provoked or enabled by the broadcast media in the following parliamentary elections (2008).[49]

JOURNALIST TRAINING PROGRAMS

Workshops can be conducted for journalists to provide training in the investigation of stories of electoral conflict. The training can include instruction on how to ask the right questions, reveal abuses and serve as a voice for the targets of conflict. As journalists may also be targets, training can also be provided in personal security techniques in conflictive electoral environments. During Armenian parliamentary by-elections (2010), reporters from Radio Free Europe/Radio Liberty – Armenia were attacked on three occasions in attempts to stop them from covering the election campaign.

TRADITIONAL LEADER PROGRAMS

If traditional leaders play a role in religious or community groups, they can be involved in programs to educate and mediate electoral disputes. For example, for the voter registration program in Bangladesh cited above, UNDP engaged mullahs and imams to support efforts for the registration of women. And, the Zimbabwe Election Support Network, a domestic CSO, is conducting the Zimbabwe Peace Project in which workshops are held in rural areas to promote reconciliation training and peace dialogues.

Traditional leaders are invited to participate in the workshops and then bring the new conflict management skills back to their villages.

In Iraq (2005) in Anbar, the Multi-National Force - West (MNF-W) engaged local tribes in electoral security. Such a partnership was not only effective in the prevention and management of electoral conflict; it also enhanced the Sunni 'ownership' of the election outcomes. Voter turnout can be one measure of effectiveness. For the January election, approximately 2 percent of the eligible voters cast ballots in Anbar province. That number increased to 38 percent for the October referendum; and, in December, there was an 86 percent turnout for the parliamentary elections and few incidents of conflict in the governorate.

MONITORING AND EVALUATION

Poll workers await voters at an indoor polling station in Bentiv Biemruok, Sudan on April 13, 2010.

The foundations for a robust M&E approach were established during the Assessment, Planning and Programming phases. Building on this information, the M&E phase of the Framework will assist with defining a performance management plan (PMP). A good PMP is critical, particularly in rapidly evolving situations, for both assessing progress against desired results and testing the validity of the development hypothesis.

INTRODUCTION TO MONITORING AND EVALUATION (M&E)

Although the monitoring and evaluation (M&E) section appears last in the Electoral Security Framework, working through the other phases – assessment, planning and programming –contributes to a strong M&E foundation.

This M&E approach is formalized in a Performance Management Plan (PMP), as required by ADS 203.3.3.[50] An effective PMP will support:.

- Measuring progress against desired program and activity results;

- Continuous testing of the validity of the development hypothesis;

- Measuring progress mitigating higher-level conflict dynamics, or, at a minimum, assessing whether your interventions are "doing harm";

- Helping USAID to "tell our story" to the U.S. Congress and American citizens.

BUILDING A PERFORMANCE MONITORING PLAN

The following table offers a quick review of M&E terminology. In some cases, particularly when working in conflict or post-conflict countries, you may

TABLE 8 MONITORING AND EVALUATION TERMINOLOGY	
Term	Definition
Development Hypothesis	How the proposed intervention will effectively address the problem.
Critical Assumptions	Assumptions underpinning the success of the program.
Program Objective	The highest level objective upon which USAID can expect to have material effect (stated as a result).
Baseline	Status prior to intervention
Target	Expected status at the end of the intervention.
Indicator	How we measure progress against objectives.
Performance Management Plan	A plan for obtaining systematic feedback on the robustness of the development hypothesis and strengthening it over time.

also hear the term "theory of change." A theory of change refers to the expected result coming from a particular set of actions.[51] It reflects the assumed connections between a set of actions and the desired result. For purposes of the Electoral Security Framework, theory of change can be considered synonymous with development hypothesis. While working through the framework, each phase yields valuable contributions to the PMP.

The electoral security assessment, ideally combined with findings from the Conflict Assessment Framework (CAF) or Inter-agency Conflict Assessment Framework (ICAF), provided information that informed:

- Broad conflict dynamics – drivers of conflict and mitigating factors (if CAF/ICAF is conducted);

- Security vulnerabilities and opportunities;

- Identification of a problem statement;

- Priorities for electoral security interventions (based on country context).

From an M&E perspective, this information will inform:

- Consideration of linkages between possible areas of program intervention and broader conflict dynamics;

- Development of an initial development hypothesis based on the identified problem statement, and critical assumptions;

- A preliminary understanding of availability and data quality for baseline data and indicators.

The electoral security planning phase informed further refinement of assessment findings by overlaying additional considerations such as identification of local change agents, international community presence and programs, and USAID interests and constraints. The planning phase provided information that informed:

- Finalized priority areas of intervention;

- Definition of program objectives and associated indicators at the objective level;

- Refined development hypothesis and critical assumptions;

- Additional information about availability and quality of data – for example, what do other donors have?;

- Consideration of a coordination approach or other means of engaging international and domestic partners.

From an M&E perspective, when reflecting on planning findings, also consider other variables that may need to be monitored, even if they fall outside of direct electoral security programming. For example, if a planned civil society voter education program depends on an organizational capacity building program undertaken by another program or donor, even though USAID may not be directly implementing, it is important to track the progress of this other program because it impacts USAID's ability to undertake activities. If the civil society program experiences delays in reaching key benchmarks, organizations may not have the necessary capacity to move forward with voter education as intended.

Next, the electoral security programming phase led to the design of an electoral security program responsive to country context and needs, factoring in the work of other domestic and international actors and reflecting USAID's interests and constraints. The rationale underlying selection of these activities is articulated in the development hypothesis.

While the ADS requires a PMP to include performance indicators, it does not specify a format. Each operating unit should design a PMP that best fits their needs.

Aside from performance indicators, a good PMP will include:

- Definition of the indicator, unit of measurement, and brief justification;

- Baseline and target values;

- Whenever possible, indicators should be disaggregated by sex;

- Data source and method of collection or calculation;

- Schedule for data collection;

- Known data limitations and how they will be addressed;

- Data quality assessment procedures;

- Cost estimate;

- Identify possible evaluation efforts;

- Calendar of performance management tasks.

Increased Stakes, Scrutiny and Number of Actors

The high-profile nature of elections, particularly as part of a peace agreement or a new constitution, is often characterized by increased stakes, scrutiny and number of actors. Electoral security programming may need to account for:

- Prominent USG political and military considerations;

- Different objectives within the USG;

- Different assumptions about how change occurs;

- Pressure to demonstrate results quickly;

- Multiple actors;

- Short time frames;

- Lack of common frame of reference – for example, place names.

From an M&E perspective, the programming phase should include:

- Conduct of a baseline before programming begins in order to test candidate indicators for accuracy and measurability, as well as to identify data that will serve as a point of departure against which to measure progress;

- Identification of performance standards – targeted indicators that identify minimum requirements for what electoral security activities hope to achieve.

At this time, many of the elements of a PMP have already been defined. Now it is important to think about pulling it all together, including an approach for collecting data, managing data, analyzing data, and making sure that managers have access to information in a timely manner to make program adjustments as necessary.

In addition to tracking progress against objectives and continuously testing the validity of the development hypothesis, a PMP helps USAID "tell its story" to the US Congress and the American people. In insecure environments, a PMP can take on even greater significance. Many of the activities implemented in these environments are experimental in nature and relatively untested compared to activities undertaken in more stable environments. It is unlikely to find a large body of lessons learned or best practices that are easily transferable to the particular context in which USAID is operating. As a result, the PMP becomes an important tool for validating (or not) the development hypothesis and program design.

When developing a PMP, keep in mind the importance of gathering information on results that are supported by other development partners. If successful implementation of USAID's activities is contingent on the timing and effectiveness of another partners' program, it will be important to monitor their progress as well.

CHALLENGES OF M&E IN INSECURE ENVIRONMENTS[52]

As referenced earlier, the Electoral Assessment Framework can be used in two types of environments: 1) otherwise stable environments where elections may trigger conflict; and 2) elections in conflict or post-conflict environments. Much literature exists on conducting M&E in stable environments; however, conducting M&E in unstable environments, including conflict and post-conflict countries, poses some unique challenges.

Rapidly changing environment: The environment often fluctuates rapidly, making planning more difficult. Security may be an inhibiting factor and demographics may shift repeatedly as people relocate. A rapidly changing environment will have implications for conducting routine data collection, as well as critical assumptions about progress in meeting performance targets. Progress may not be steadily incremental, but rather move forward in spurts depending on security and other factors. In addition, the key assumptions underpinning the development hypothesis may change repeatedly, necessitating continuous assessment and the flexibility to adjust.

Less transparency: People may be less willing to be open and honest regarding issues perceived as sources of vulnerability. What motivates behavior may not be as clear as in more stable environments.

Lack of trust: Information gathering may be hindered by a fear of reprisals or distrust of outsiders.

Instability: Lack of security can impede activity implementation and interrupt routine data gathering.

Lack of reliable and accessible data: Particularly following prolonged conflict, there may be a dearth of reliable and accessible data. This will have an impact on baseline data collection and formulation of indicators. Data may simply not exist. When it does, depending on the source, reliability of data may be contested by different parties to the conflict. Governments or others may attempt to impede access to sources of information, such as certain regions of the country or ethnic groups.

Extreme weakness of host country institutions: Following prolonged conflict, government and civil society organizations are likely to be very weak. They will likely need capacity building support to become partners in monitoring and evaluation.

Challenges of attribution and causality: Attribution refers to the causal linkages between expected or observed changes and specific program activities. In environments characterized by lack of transparency, rapid change, and multiple actors, attribution and causality can be difficult to determine. There may not always be a direct cause and effect relationship.

Physical security of evaluators and informants: In addition to the challenges of inaccessibility posed by insecure environments, the security of evaluators and staff is of paramount importance. Evaluators may be vulnerable as outsiders in a community. Likewise, informants may be targeted for speaking or associating with outsiders.

In addition to the challenges of operating in insecure environments, the high-profile nature of elections is likely to lead to increased stakes, scrutiny and number of actors operating in the electoral security arena. This will be especially true if elections are part of a peace agreement or a new constitution and there is significant U.S. foreign policy interest in the country and election outcomes (see Increased Stakes, Scrutiny and Number of Actors). [53]

GOOD PRACTICES FOR CONDUCTING M&E IN INSECURE ENVIRONMENTS[54]

General M&E best practices, and accounting for the challenges above, will form the basis for conducting M&E in insecure environments.

Monitor progress against electoral security results and conflict dynamics: Electoral security indicators will monitor efficiency, effectiveness, impact and sustainability of the program. Conflict indicators will monitor progress against conflict dynamics.

Focus on manageable interests: Selected program objectives and indicators should demonstrate the causal effect of the intervention. Manageable interests are things that USAID can realistically impact through its interventions. The program objective is the highest level expression of manageable interests.

Ensure that indicator data exists: When considering candidate indicators, make sure that the data is reliable and available. This can be tested when conducting a baseline assessment. Indicators informed by poor quality data will not be useful. Similarly, if the data is not readily available, the cost of collection may outweigh the value of the indicator. Where direct indicators are not available, consider a carefully selected proxy.

Triangulate and build in redundancies: When availability and quality of data are questionable, it is important to triangulate or to integrate various sources and methods of data collection. Also build in redundancies. If people are hesitant to share information, ask the same question in different ways and compare responses. Be inclined to oversample to ensure that groups not included, perhaps due to security concerns, are accounted for in other areas. Collect data from different sources and use multiple data collection methods to balance out data weakness.

Use clusters of indicators for a given outcome: Clusters of indicators will help to capture different time frames and balance differences between perception and actual performance. USAID uses a combination of standard and custom indicators for reporting purposes (see Standard and Custom Indicators). In the initial stages of a program, output rather than outcome indicators provide effective and legitimate monitoring measures during early stabilization efforts. As the program continues, outcome indicators will assume increasing importance.

Combine qualitative and quantitative indicators: In insecure environments, public perception takes on heightened importance. Formal channels of communication may have broken down, leaving people to act on perceptions. It is important to track public perception, but equally important to balance it with measures of actual change.

Recognize the importance of contextual indicators: Contextual indicators take on increasing importance, particularly after prolonged conflict. The way things 'should' work has likely broken down, resulting in shifts in power dynamics and even values. Context may also have an impact on the progress of interventions and selection of proxy indicators.

Establish consensus on metrics early: When possible, work with partners to establish consensus on program objectives and metrics. This will help to clarify respective roles and support coordination with other programs. In the event that baseline data is missing, work with partners to establish consensus on a baseline and how it was measured.

Use local and international partners: In highly insecure environments where physical access to sites may not be possible, consider use of technology applications for M&E. For example, aerial photography and GPS coordinates may be used to verify location of polling stations, track population movements, etc. If present, the US military often has the technology and the capacity to support this type of monitoring. Furthermore, the use of picture phones, SMS technology, and web-based technologies can be used in environments where there may be environmental, personnel or security impediments to traditional data collection.

Budget for M&E: In addition to factoring the development of a PMP, data collection, analysis and other direct M&E expenses into the budget, also allow for training of local staff engaged in M&E. Unstable environments are often characterized by high staff turnover. Make sure that building in redundancies extends to M&E staff.

USAID uses both Standard and Custom Indicators for reporting purposes. Standard indicators for elections and political process include:

- Number of election officials trained with USG assistance;

- Number of people reached by USG-assisted voter education;

- Number of laws or amendments to ensure credible elections drafted with USG technical assistance.

Custom indicators are tailored to specific programs and contexts. For elections and political process, custom indicators may include:

- Degree of independence of electoral authority;

- Incidents of electoral violence, disaggregated;

- Level of voter confidence in electoral authority;

- Level of acceptance of results by losers.

ELECTORAL SECURITY FRAMEWORK TOOLKIT

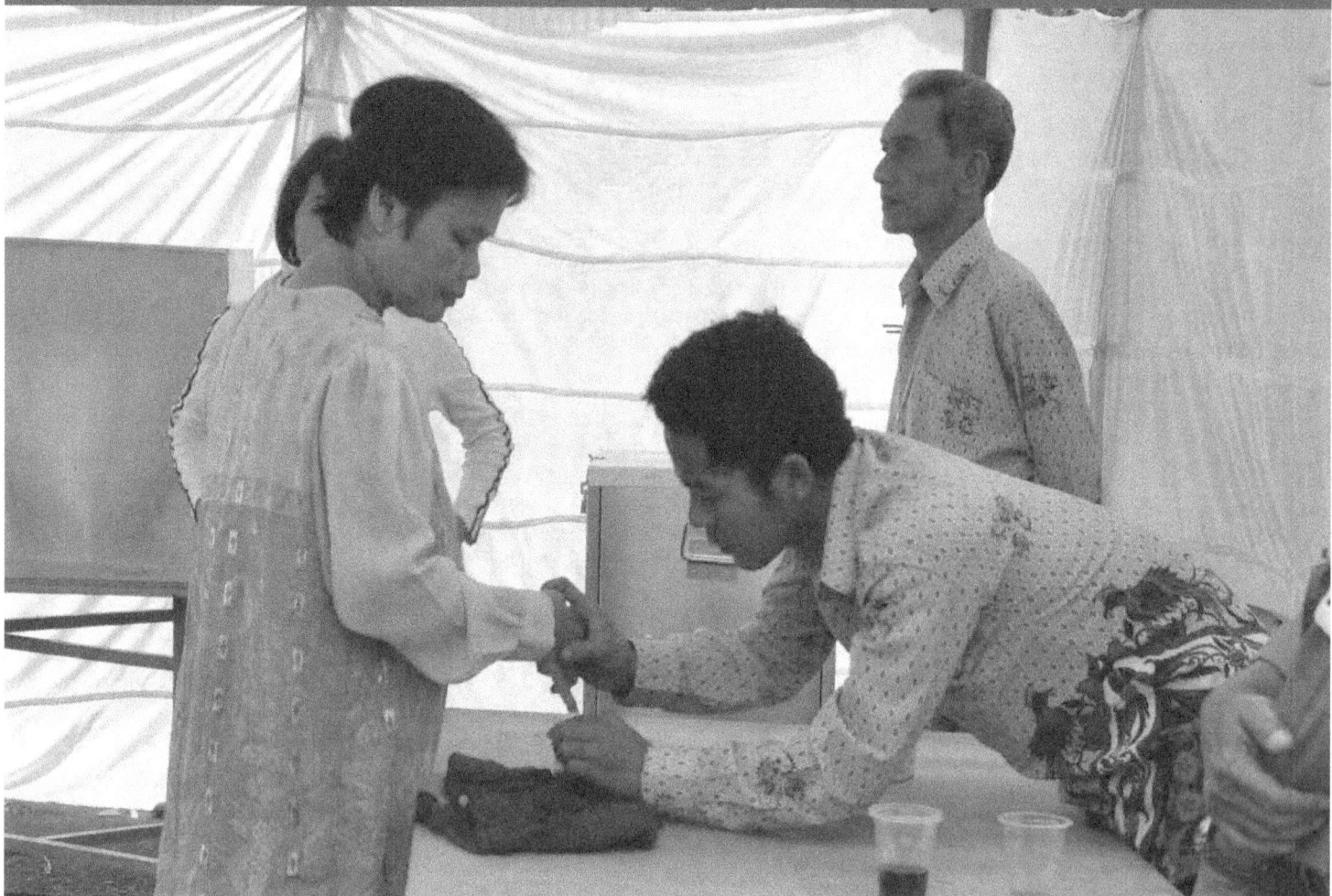

To prevent multiple voting, an Indonesian woman is marked with indelible ink after voting in the July 2009 presidential elections.

PURPOSE

The purpose of an Electoral Security Assessment Toolkit (the Toolkit) is to provide policy-makers and practitioners with a comprehensive, systematic and actionable approach to profiling potential electoral conflict so that appropriate development hypotheses and programming can be formulated to prevent, manage or mediate the conflict. The Toolkit outlined below seeks to be consistent with approaches already developed by CMM and its CAF and complies with the principles of the ICAF, applying these to an electoral context.

USAID conflict assessment "diagnostic tools" assist USAID Missions to address issues in the following three areas:

- Identify and prioritize the causes and consequences of violence and instability that are most important in a given country context;

- Understand how existing development programs interact with these factors;

- Determine where development and humanitarian assistance can most effectively support local efforts to manage conflict and build peace.[55]

If a CAF or an ICAF have been conducted, these assessments should be consulted in order to identify the contextual drivers of conflict, mitigating factors, vulnerabilities and opportunities. The Conflict Equation of the CAF is shown below:

Motives + Means + Opportunity = Conflict

The CAF explores the underlying causes linked to potential conflict including:

- Causes that fuel incentives or motives for participation in violence such as grievance or greed;

- Causes that facilitate the mobilization and expansion of violence through access to resources;

- Causes found at the level of state and social capacity to manage and respond to violence;

- Regional or international causes resulting from globalization or bad neighborhoods.

Building upon the identification of causes, the CAF will examine the motives, means and opportunities for conflict to be triggered in the overall conflict dynamics of the country.

The ICAF identifies the "windows of vulnerability" and "windows of opportunity" for conflict emergence or prevention. The ICAF lists an election as the first example of a window of vulnerability and states: "Elections are the most obvious example, but any type of change that threatens to alter established patterns of political or economic control in high-risk environments could lead elites to mobilize violence."[56] To ensure harmony between US programming and approach, the Toolkit outlined below applies the CAF and ICAF concepts to electoral conflict prevention, management and mediation. The Toolkit will inform the problem statement, development hypothesis and definition of the electoral conflict.

In preparing for the electoral security assessment, other USAID country assessments should be consulted including DG, economic growth, gender and environment. DG Officers or their designees may conduct an electoral security assessment. An assessment team should consist of an electoral specialist, a conflict specialist and a country expert. The Mission can include the assessment findings into its larger set of portfolios for EPP and CMM programming. Concerning planning, the assessment should be conducted at least 18 months prior to Election Day. The combination of desk research and field interviews should take around three weeks to complete. Since the potential for conflict can emerge in the early electoral phases, early assessments offer the advantage of developing full electoral cycle programs and can benefit from the relationships, building blocks and synergies that emerge over the course of time.

ELECTORAL SECURITY FRAMEWORK TOOLKIT

The Toolkit is composed of three sets of elements: 1) historical conflict factors; 2) contextual analysis; 3) stakeholder analysis (state and non-state).

HISTORICAL CONFLICT FACTORS

- Obtain a profile of past electoral conflict. This is essential to creating a current electoral threat profile. Research suggests that past experience of electoral conflict is a predictor of future conflict.

- Examine the nature and magnitude of previous electoral conflict. This conflict should be described in relation to any larger conflict dynamic in the country such as a recent civil war.

- Profile on-going insurgencies and rebellions in terms of the nature of the grievances, length of time, number of militants and locations of conflict.

- Conflict factor analyses should include a description of criminality in the country through reported crime statistics.

- Describe the traditional roles of the military and police in elections and their rules of engagement.

- The scale of 0 to 3, as shown in the Historical Conflict section, can measure the level of violence by quantifying electoral conflict by type and timing of incidents. In this case 0 represents the absence of conflict and 3 represents conflict involving the loss of life of 20 or more persons.

CONTEXTUAL ANALYSIS

POLITICAL RISK FACTORS

- Describe the legal architecture governing the elections and security arrangements including constitutional provisions, legislation, regulations and administrative procedures. If a peace agreement is being implemented, describe the electoral terms of the agreement.

- Describe the regime's Freedom House rating (Free, Partly Free or Not Free) and the accompanying rating number.

- Describe the USAID country classification of

The development of an ICAF-based Conflict Prevention Plan includes the following steps:

- Specify current USG activities;

- Specify current efforts of non-USG actors;

- Identify drivers of conflict and mitigating factors;

- Specify challenges to address the gaps;

- Referring to Windows of Vulnerability, describe risks associated with failure to address the Gaps; and

- Referring to Windows of Opportunity, identify the opportunities to address the gaps.[1]

either a New and Fragile Democracy; Authoritarian or Semi-Authoritarian State; or Crisis and Rebuilding Society.

ECONOMIC RISK FACTORS

- Countries where the average per capita income is lower than $2,700 per year may be at greater risk of electoral conflict than in countries where the income is higher.

- Inequities in wealth and land distribution are also vulnerabilities. Conditions associated with GINI indexes greater than 50.0 may contribute to electoral conflict.

- Smaller economies may also be vulnerabilities with electoral conflict tending to occur in those economies less than $100 billion (USD) per year.

SOCIAL RISK FACTORS

- Map social cleavages and the impact of religious, ethnic, linguistic or regional divides on electoral competition and conflict.

- Identify recent migration patterns that have altered the demographics of a given geographical area.

- Calculate the number of individuals aged 15 to 24 and the percentage of the total population as represented by this age group.

- Describe the role of elites in past elections.

- Map the diaspora, identify their electoral rights and describe their interactions with homeland groups.

STATE INSTITUTION RISK FACTORS

- Assess the capacity of the institutions to fulfill its statutory mandates.

- Identify any "politicized" elements within the institutions and ascertain if state resources are being employed for political purposes.

- Describe institutional gaps where the state is failing to protect or include a location or a segment of the electorate.

- Describe the rules of engagement for crowd control and polling station protection by security forces and determine if it is excessive or insufficiently robust.

- Identify illicit power structures within state institutions that yield command and veto authority over conventional governance processes.

ELECTION-SPECIFIC RISK FACTORS

- Identify the electoral system in order to assess its impact on conflict, if any. Systems can be broadly identified as Majoritarian/Plurality, Proportional or Mixed. If there is a delimitation process, identify what authority draws the district boundaries and when boundaries are to be redrawn.

- Describe the role of the executive in governance, whether a presidential system or not.

- Describe whether it is a federal or unitary state and the decentralization arrangements.

- Identify the number of registered political parties and their profiles. Political party registration requirements and political finance disclosure requirements should be included.

- Describe the electoral dispute resolution mechanisms and the public perceptions about fairness and effectiveness of these mechanisms.

- Evaluate the structural and behavioral independence of the EMB.

- Describe the potential impact of the timing and sequencing of elections on conflict.

- Concerning recent elections, describe the observer and news reports about vote fraud.

- Note whether there is a boycott of the election by a party, group of parties, regional or ethnic group and the reason for this boycott.

- Ascertain if campaign activity regulations contribute to conflict by opening up unregulated opportunities for political confrontation to occur.

- Identify the avenues for hate speech to be disseminated and the role of rumor in societal exchanges and suspicions.

- Evaluate the level of usage, type of user and kind of new media technology available in the country such as SMS texting, social networking sites and telephone video recording.

- If this is the first election following major political or governmental reform, describe the reforms and the expectations surrounding it.

Annex I is an Historical and Contextual Factors Worksheet. At the conclusion of the contextual analysis, this worksheet can be completed to identify factors that are potential vulnerabilities for electoral conflict.

STAKEHOLDER ANALYSIS

The state stakeholders are regulatory, security, judicial, and public administrative in nature. The state institution matrix is shown in the table below.

Non-state stakeholders include political parties, civil society organizations, media organizations and traditional leaders. Non-state stakeholders also include private security companies and community-based watch committees. Non-state spoilers may include political party activists, media organizations, insurgents, rebels and criminals. Diasporas can play pivotal roles as spoilers or peacebuilders. This list of state and non-state stakeholders forms the basis of potential subjects for in-person assessment interviews.

In profiling electoral conflict, motives reveal the underlying incentives of the spoilers for conflict. While motives are contextual, their common objective is to achieve some political aim – influencing selections and turnout, enhancing bargaining positions or changing demographics. The motives could involve an economic dimension, such as the rents and patronage from public resources associated with electoral victory.

Once identified or surmised, these motives should be matched with electoral spoilers. The capacities and the access to conflict resources for the following categories of electoral spoilers should be identified:

- State and State Proxies;

- Coalitions of Opposition Parties;

- Political Rivals;

- Insurgents and Rebels;

- Criminals.

In the USAID CMM "stakeholder analysis" of individuals and organizations capable of transforming grievances into violence, six basic questions are employed:

- Who are the actors?

- What is their role in the pattern?

- What is the rationale for their grievances?

- What are their resources and capacities?

- How can they be engaged?

- What are their priorities?[57]

Annex I also shows a Spoiler/Motive Evaluation Worksheet. This Worksheet can guide the assessment in identifying the kinds of spoilers that may emerge during the election and what their possible motives for conflict may be.

Electoral spoilers will identify and aim to compromise specific targets. Human targets include voters, candidates, election officials, security forces, election observers and media representatives. The gender, age and ethnic background of the victims should be noted. Information targets include sensitive materials such as ballots and paper registries as well as computerized registries and ballot tabulations. Facility

TABLE 9 STATE ELECTORAL SECURITY MATRIX			
Regulatory Institutions	Security Institutions	Judicial Institutions	Public Administration Institutions
Legislative Committees	International and National Military	Supreme Courts	Civil Registries
EMBs	International, National and Local Police Forces	High Courts	Education Ministries
Media Commissions		Constitutional Courts	Social Service Agencies
Land and Boundary Commissions	Community-Based Watch Committees	Ordinary Courts	Sub-National Governments
Anti-Corruption Commissions		Electoral Dispute Resolution Mechanisms	
		Transitional Justice Mechanisms	

targets include registration and polling sites, election offices, party and candidate offices, and residences and hotels for candidates, observers and media. And, event targets include official activities such as voter registration drives or voter education sessions, and political events like campaign rallies, debates and internal party leadership meetings.

The tactics employed against these targets must be profiled. This profile should include a description of the type of assault – intimidation, physical injury, torture, sexual assault, strategic displacement or murder. The type of weapon, if any, should be identified. If property is targeted, then the profile should describe the extent of vandalism, damage or arson that has occurred.

A Target Evaluation Worksheet is shown in Annex I. This Worksheet can guide the assessment in identifying possible targets for conflict and the likelihood that they will become victims.

Conflict can occur in any phase of the electoral cycle. For the purposes of the assessment, the following divisions in the electoral cycle can be employed:

- Phase 1: The long run-up to electoral events (18 months to three months prior)

- Phase 2: The campaign's final lap (three months prior to election day)

- Phase 3: Polling day(s)

- Phase 4: Between voting and proclamation

- Phase 5: Post-election outcomes and their aftermath[58]

An Electoral Cycle Conflict Worksheet is shown in Annex I. This Worksheet overlays potential conflict with a phase in the electoral cycle. It guides the assessment in identifying the potential for conflict in different phases of the electoral calendar.

Locations of possible conflict should be profiled. Regional or provincial areas should be assigned vulnerability ratings (low, medium and high) based upon past violence, proximity to conflict zones, crime rates or other factors influencing the level of conflict in that location. High threat locations can be designated as 'hot spots.' Maps and databases can be developed to identify the locations where incidents occurred, when they occurred and what tactics were employed. Using this database, the intensity of the conflict can be measured in each phase of the electoral cycle.

STAKEHOLDER QUESTIONS

Below are sets of questions that can be posed to and about stakeholders for the assessment.

STATE STAKEHOLDER QUESTIONS

REGULATORY INSTITUTIONS

Legislatures
- What are the key instruments that form the legal architecture?
- Which legislative committees are responsible for drafting electoral laws?
- Are electoral reform measures in process? If so, describe the reforms.
- Are there aspects of existing legislation that create electoral risks?
- Are there aspects of the law or institutional resiliencies that mitigate risks?
- If a peace agreement is being implemented, what are the electoral terms of the agreement?

EMBs
- Does the EMB have structural independence from the government in legislation and finance?
- How is the EMB appointed and what do its members represent, i.e., political parties, judiciary, or civil society?
- Have recent opinion polls been conducted to measure the public's perceptions about the performance of the EMB?
- Does the EMB receive electoral assistance from the international community? If so, please describe.
- How have recent election observation reports evaluated the technical efficiency and democratic quality of electoral administration?
- What role does the EMB play in electoral security administration?
- What has been the nature of complaints filed against the EMB in past elections?
- Have any election officials been targeted for intimidation or violence during past elections? If so, who were the perpetrators, what did they do, when and where did they do it? How did the perpetrators obtain their conflict resources?

Media, Land and Boundary, Anti-Corruption Commissions
- Does the Commission have structural independence from the government in legislation and finance?
- Media – has the commission played an effective role in assuring accuracy in broadcast and print content and equitable access to media time and space for qualified political entities?
- Land and Boundary – do the constituency boundaries reflect international principles of respecting existing administration units, taking into account geographical features and allowing for representation by communities of interest?
- Anti-Corruption – what is the record of the commission in uncovering corruption in political finance? What penalties have been issued against parties for infractions?
- Do any of the commissions receive electoral assistance from the international community? If so, please describe.

SECURITY INSTITUTIONS

International Military
- What is the electoral mandate of the international military force?

- Outside of this mandate, what additional role will forces play in security, logistics and communications?

- Is there a Quick Reaction Force?

- How is electoral security enforcement coordinated with other agencies?

National Military
- Are security sector reforms planned or underway?

- What is the role of the national military in election administration?

- How is electoral security enforcement coordinated with other agencies?

- If there is no role, where will the forces be garrisoned?

- Do members of the military have the right to vote? If so, when and where do they cast their ballots?

- Has the military ever performed a coup d'état? If so, when did it occur and what is its impact on the current election?

National Police
- Is there a national police or constabulary force?

- If so, how will the police be deployed – mobile, fixed or reserve?

- What are their rules of engagement for crowd control?

- How is electoral security enforcement coordinated with other agencies?

- Have the national police been trained in electoral security by the international community?

Local Police
- If there are local police, how will they be deployed – mobile, fixed, or reserve?

- Are the local police armed?

- What are their rules of engagement?

- What are the demographics of the police force in terms of ethnic and gender composition?

- How is electoral security enforcement coordinated with other agencies?

- Do the local police operate detention facilities?

- Are local police assisted by other official or quasi-official grassroots security entities such as village watches or patrols?

- How is electoral security enforcement coordinated with other agencies?

- Have the national police been trained in electoral security by the international community?

JUDICIAL INSTITUTIONS

High, Supreme and Constitutional Courts
- Are high courts considered independent from the government?

- In past elections, have high courts been employed to determine the outcomes of an election or the eligibility of major candidates?

- If so, what parties brought the complaints to the high court for redress?

Electoral Tribunals and Special Electoral Courts
- Is there a special tribunal or court that hears electoral cases?

- If so, is that tribunal or court separate from the EMB?

- Do citizens consider these courts credible? Are these legal channels used by citizens?

- How is this court appointed and who are its members?

- What kinds of cases has the tribunal or court heard in recent elections and what were their decisions?

Ordinary Courts
- Are ordinary courts considered as independent from the government?

- Have ordinary courts been employed to hear electoral complaints of a criminal nature? If so, what has been the experience in providing justice?

- Do ordinary courts have any authority to overturn election results or call for a new election?

Transitional Justice
- Were there widespread human rights abuses in recent elections?

- If so, was there an investigation or any transitional justice undertaken?

- Were perpetrators of the abuses identified and penalized?

- Was there any compensation or redress for the victims of the abuses?

PUBLIC ADMINISTRATION INSTITUTIONS

Government ministry officials

- Are officials appointed or elected?

- If appointed, who are they appointed by and under what terms?

Government ministry bodies, at the national and local level

- What is the relationship among different ministries?

- Which ministries really hold power and which are beholden to other actors?

- What role have ministries played in past elections?

- What is the relationship between ministries and the political parties?

- Have certain powerful officials placed pressure on other ministers or staff to vote certain ways or are they associated with any political party?

- Have ministries with election-related responsibilities performed effectively and efficiently in past elections?

- Do civil servants and appointed officials act as extensions of the ruling party during elections rather than non-partisan public servants?

- Do they interpret their functions in a politicized manner?

- Do they act with party interests in mind rather than taking a non-partisan approach?

- Are they expected to belong to a certain political party and vote a certain way? Are there prohibitions on civil servants from advocating for political parties?

Sub-national governments

- Characterize the relationships among different levels of government. To what extent is government decentralized?

- Are sub-national governments wholly dependent on the national government for resource transfers or do they have some capacity at the sub-national level to raise and allocate funds?

- If so, do they have security responsibilities at the sub-national level?

- Are security forces beholden to local-level officials?

NON-STATE STAKEHOLDER QUESTIONS

Civil Society Organizations
- How are civil society organizations registered and regulated by the government?

- Can civil society organizations receive financial grants from international organizations?

- What is the mission of the civil society organization?

- Does the organization receive electoral assistance from the international community? If so, please describe.

- What are the influences of elites on the organization's activities?

- Does the organization have a diaspora- affiliated branch?

- In what parts of the country does the organization conduct programming?

- For electoral purposes, is this organization in a network or coalition with other likeminded organizations?

- Is the civil society organization connected to any political party?

- What activities are planned during the election?

- Have any of the organization's representatives been targeted for intimidation or violence during past elections? If so, who were the perpetrators, what did they do, when and where did they do it? How did the perpetrators obtain their conflict resources?

- Have offices or residences of the organization's leadership ever been the target of attack?

Political Parties
- How are political parties registered with the government and what are the eligibility requirements?

- What are the obligations of parties to disclose contributions and expenditures of party, candidate and campaign funds?

- Does the party receive electoral assistance from the international community? If so, please describe.

- Does this party have a constitution and statement of principles?

- Does this party occupy seats in parliament? On the sub-national level? What is the party's position on the type of electoral system in place and the fairness of any delimitation that has been conducted?

- Does the party have any ties to neighboring countries or affiliations with likeminded parties in those countries?

- Have party representatives been targeted for intimidation or violence in recent elections? If so, who were the perpetrators, what did they do, when did they do it? How did the perpetrators obtain their conflict resources?

- Have offices or residences of party leadership ever been the target of attack?

- Has the party signed a code of conduct?

- How does this party communicate with other parties? Is there a national council of party representatives? If not, would this party participate in one if it is established?

Media Organizations

- Are there both private and government operated media in the country?

- How are private media organizations licensed by the government?

- Does the organization receive electoral assistance from the international community? If so, please describe.

- Otherwise, from what sources does the media organization receive its revenues?

- How does news coverage of the election differ between international and domestic media reports?

- Does this organization represent a political party or mainly espouse the views of a particular party?

- Are the activities and access to the media regulated by the same authority or commission? If so, how is government-operated media regulated?

- What are the regulations on equitable access to broadcasting for political parties?

- Has the organization ever been accused of disseminating misinformation or provocative rhetoric?

- Have journalists been targeted for intimidation or violence? If so, who were the perpetrators, what did they do, when and where did they do it? How did the perpetrators obtain their conflict resources?

- Have any of offices or residences of the organization's leadership ever been the target of attack?

Traditional Leaders

- What kinds of traditional leaders may play roles in the elections? Religious? Tribal? Community? Other identity based factors?

- How do they become traditional leaders?

- Is their role largely ceremonial or do they provide services for their communities?

- Is their position recognized by the State?

- Is there a dominant community, competitive communities or are there many communities fragmented across the country?

- What roles have traditional leaders played in past elections? Education? Mediation? Peace-building within and among communities? What are the trends in their leadership? That is, are traditional leader growing more or less influential?

- Do traditional leaders have more influence in rural areas or certain regions?

- Have traditional leaders been subject to manipulation or coercion by the ruling party, elites or economic interests?

- Has their community been subject to discrimination or strategic displacement for electoral purposes?

- Have traditional leaders or members of their communities been targeted for intimidation or violence in recent elections? If so, who were the perpetrators, what did they do, when and where did they do it?

Private Security Companies
- Is the State where programming is being conducted a signatory to the 2008 Montreux Document on private security companies?

- What are the company's security responsibilities and under what contract are these responsibilities described?

- Have any of the company's representatives been injured or killed in an electoral attack?

- Have any of the company representatives fired rounds in electoral security enforcement and, if so, what was the result?

Insurgents and Rebels
- What is the nature of the insurgency, that is, what is the grievance of the insurgents against the status quo?

- How long has the insurgency been in existence? What is the estimated size?

- In what parts of the country is the insurgency particularly strong or weak?

- What is the role of women in the insurgency?

- From what sources does the insurgency obtain its funds?

- Is the leadership of the insurgency centralized around a handful of figures or decentralized and devolved in management?

- What are its methods of recruiting new insurgents?

- What are the tactics of the insurgency? (i.e. Car bombs? Kidnappings? Political assassinations?)

- What is the level of community support for the insurgency?

Criminals
- If crime statistics are available, what are the rates for violent crimes?

- Are estimates available for the number of illegal small arms in the country?

- Do criminal interests engage in financially supporting political candidates or intimidating others?

- Are candidates required to publicly report their donors?

- Are the criminals involved in elections solo operators working independently on the local level or larger organized syndicates operating regionally or nationally?

- How do these criminals obtain their funds? Narcotics? Other trafficking? Skimming from extractive industries?

- Are these criminal influences in elections new phenomena or historically or family rooted?

DEVELOPMENT HYPOTHESIS

The findings of the assessment identify the priority areas for electoral interventions and allow for the definition of a development hypothesis. The development hypothesis should be focused on strengthening the institutions and processes in the electoral security system – the legal architecture, state stakeholders and non-state stakeholders. The development hypothesis should be strategic and seek to combine, leverage and synergize different program activities. The development hypothesis should be time sensitive, reflecting the fact that different threats will emerge at different points in the electoral cycle. And, the development hypothesis should remain flexible, recognizing that conflict dynamics change and programming must be adapted accordingly.

ELECTORAL SECURITY PROGRAM MATRIX

With the development hypothesis defined, the DG Officer should create a programming strategy to prevent, manage and mediate electoral conflict. A menu of programming options is shown in the matrix below. These program examples are intended to provide stakeholder-specific activities intended to leverage opportunities to prevent or diminish vulnerabilities for electoral conflict. Program and candidate indicators should be developed to measure the effectiveness of the program strategy

TABLE 10 ELECTORAL SECURITY PROGRAM MATRIXES			
STATE INSTITUTION PROGRAMMING			
REGULATORY INSTITUTIONS			
Stakeholders	Prevention	Management	Mediation
Legislatures	Electoral reform Security sector reform	Electoral reform Security sector reform	Electoral dispute resolution reform
EMBs	Legal reform Codes of Conduct for EMB officials and staff General technical assistance and capacity building to develop independence and legitimacy Targeted technical assistance to remedy a deficiency that could become conflictive	Development of electoral security administration capacity Media monitoring unit Joint Election Operations Centers Joint Election Security Task Forces Poll worker training on conflict resolution techniques	EMB/political party liaison committees
Other Regulatory Institutions	Legal reform Codes of Conduct for officials and staff General technical assistance and capacity building to develop independence and legitimacy		

SECURITY INSTITUTIONS			
Stakeholders	Prevention	Management	Mediation
Police – National and Local	Security Sector Reform Codes of Conduct Election security training programs Rules of engagement training	Fixed, mobile and reserve enforcement.	Incident mapping and analysis Fixed, mobile and reserve enforcement
Police – International	Codes of Conduct Election security training programs Rules of engagement	Fixed, mobile and reserve enforcement Technical assistance to national forces Monitoring national police forces	Incident mapping and analysis Fixed, mobile and reserve enforcement
Military – National	Security Sector Reform Codes of Conduct Election security training programs Rules of engagement training	Fixed, mobile and reserve enforcement Logistics	Incident mapping and analysis Fixed, mobile and reserve enforcement
Military – International	Codes of Conduct Electoral security training programs Rules of engagement training	Fixed, mobile and reserve enforcement Monitoring national military forces Logistics	Incident mapping and analysis Fixed, mobile and reserve enforcement
JUDICIAL INSTITUTIONS			
Stakeholders	Prevention	Management	Mediation
EMBs			Technical assistance and capacity building for election dispute resolution
National Judiciary, and Ordinary Courts			Technical assistance and capacity building for election dispute resolution Pursuing court cases against offenders
Electoral Dispute Resolution Mechanisms			Technical assistance and capacity building for election dispute resolution
Transitional Justice			Pursuing investigations, court cases and other instruments against offenders

PUBLIC ADMINISTRATIVE INSTITUTIONS			
Stakeholders	Prevention	Management	Mediation
Civil Registries	Capacity building for voter registries		
Education Ministries	Peace education courses	School security at Polling Centers	
Social Service Agencies		Humanitarian services Legal aid programs Enfranchisement of displaced or un-settled populations	
Sub-National Governments	Local civil registry capacity building		

NON-STATE PROGRAMMING			
Stakeholders	Prevention	Management	Mediation
Civil Society Organizations	Training in ADR techniques Peace committees and educational; initiatives	Legal aid services Medical and psycho-logical assistance Diaspora outreach programs	Electoral mediation Monitoring electoral conflict Monitoring electoral dispute resolution Monitoring political party code compliance Monitoring delimitation Media monitoring Peace education programming
Political Parties	Codes of Conduct Pre-election peace pacts	Political Party Councils Political party resource assistance	Political Party Councils EMB/party liaison committees Police/party liaison committees
Media Organizations	Codes of Conduct	Agreement on election reporting protocols	Monitoring campaign activities for hate speech and potential conflict
Traditional Leaders	Pre-election media-tion and education	Get-Out-The-Vote initiatives	Post-election ADR
Private Security Companies	Codes of Conduct Election security training programs	Fixed, mobile and reserve enforcement	Incident mapping and analysis Fixed, mobile and reserve enforcement
Community-Based Watch Committees	Election security training programs	Mobile and fixed enforcement	Fixed, mobile and reserve enforcement

ANNEX I: TOOLKIT WORKSHEETS

ANNEX I.1: HISTORICAL AND CONTEXTUAL FACTORS WORKSHEET

HISTORICAL AND CONTEXTUAL FACTORS WORKSHEET			
Context	Not Relevant	Possible Vulnerabilities	Likely Vulnerabilities
History of Conflict			
History of Electoral Conflict			
Post-Conflict Environment			
On-Going Insurgency or Rebellion			
Crime Rate			
Security Forces and Elections			
Political Context			
Regime Type			
Role of Executive			
Federalism and Decentralization			
Electoral System			
Political Party System			
Electoral Dispute Resolution			
EMB Independence			
Timing and Sequence of Elections			
Election Following Reforms			
Economic Context			
Per Capita Income			
GINI Index			
GDP			
Social Context			
Social Cleavages			
Migration Patterns/ Demographics			
Youth Bulge			
Role of Elites			
Role of Diaspora			

Structural Context			
Regional Conflict Dynamics			
Vote Fraud			
Electoral Boycotts			
Political Confrontations			
Channels for Hate Speech			
New Media			

ANNEX I.2: SPOILER/MOTIVE EVALUATION WORKSHEET

Spoiler/Motive Evaluation Worksheet					
Spoiler	Motive	Description	Not Likely	Possible	Very Likely
State and State Proxies	Maintaining government power	State and state proxies may employ state resources to engage in conflict to assure its return to power			
Coalitions of Opposition Parties	Overturning disputed election outcomes	Coalition of opposition parties, adversaries during the election, engage in mass-based actions to protest an election outcome			
Political Rivals	Political competition	Political rivals engage in conflict in order to gain political advantage in the contest for votes			
Insurgents	Delay, discredit, or derail the election	Insurgents do not seek success in contesting the election, but rather, in taking actions to compromise voter turnout, election administration, and the credibility of the election			
Criminals	Corruption of governance to their advantage	Criminals engage in bribery, intimidation, and violence to capture candidates and elected officials to ensure that local government does not disrupt its criminal pursuits			

TARGET EVALUATION WORKSHEET			
Target	Not Likely	Possible	Very Likely
People			
Voters			
Incumbent Candidates/Party			
Opposition Candidates/Party			
Election Officials			
Poll Workers			
Security Forces			
Election Observers			
Media Representatives			
Sensitive Materials			
Un-Voted Ballots			
Voted Ballots			
Voter Registries			
Facilities			
Election Headquarters			
Police Stations/Military Bases			
Political Party Headquarters			
Registration/Polling Centers			
Election Observer Offices			
Hotels with Observers			
Information			
Dis-Information			
Events			
Voter Registration Drives			
Campaign Rallies			
Political Party Meetings			
Poll Worker Training Sessions			

ELECTORAL CYCLE CONFLICT EVALUATION WORKSHEET				
Phase	Targets	Not Likely	Possible	Very Likely
Pre-Election	Legislatures considering election laws			
	Election planning facilities			
	Police stations			
	Voter registration sites			
	Refugee/IDP repatriation centers			
	Other			
Campaign	Political party offices			
	Rallies			
	Debates			
	Other			
Election Day	Election offices			
	Polling Centers			
	Counting Centers			
	Police Stations			
	Political party offices			
	Media offices			
	Other			
Post-Election/Pre-Announcement	Election offices			
	Police stations			
	Political party offices			
	Electoral justices offices			
	Other			
Announcement of Results	Election offices			
	Political stations			
	Political Party Offices			
	Electoral justice offices			
	Other			

ANNEX II: ACRONYMS

ACE	Administration and Cost of Elections (ACE) Electoral Knowledge Network
ADR	Alternative Dispute Resolution
AGE	Anti-Government Elements
AOR	Area of Responsibility
AU	African Union
BEC	Bangladesh Election Commission
BEC	Bureau Electoral Communal (Haiti)
BED	Bureau Electoral Departmental (Haiti)
CAF	Conflict Assessment Framework
CEP	Conseil Electoral Provisoire (Haiti)
CD	Democratic Convergence Party (El Salvador)
CGTF	Citizens' Goodwill Task Force (Guinea-Bissau)
CMC	Code Monitoring Commission (Sierra Leone)
CMM	Office of Conflict Management and Mitigation (USAID)
COMELEC	Commission on Elections (Philippines)
CPP	Cambodian People's Party
CSO	Civil Society Organization
CVEM	Centre for Monitoring Electoral Violence (Sri Lanka)
DCMC	District Code Monitoring Committees (Sierra Leone)
DDR	Disarmament, Demobilization and Reintegration
DFID	Department for International Development (UK)
DG	Office of Democracy and Governance (USAID)
DPA	Democratic Party of Albanians
DUI	Democratic Union of Integration (Albania)
EASC	Electoral Appeals Sub-commission (Bosnia and Herzegovina)
ECAC	Electoral Complaints and Appeals Sub-commission (Kosovo)
ECC	Electoral Complaints Commission (Afghanistan)
ECI	Election Commission of India
EMB	Election Management Body
ERG	Election Response Group (Kosovo)
ESWG	Election Security Working Group (Bosnia and Herzegovina)
EU	European Union
EVER	Electoral Violence Education and Resolution Program
FARC	Fuerzas Armadas Revolucionarias de Colombia
GPPP	Ghana Political Parties' Program
GSI	Global Security Industry
HNP	Haitian National Police
ICAF	Interagency Conflict Assessment Framework
ICC	International Criminal Court
ICITAP	International Criminal Investigation Training Assistance Program (U.S. Department of Justice)
IDEA	Institute for Democracy and Electoral Assistance
IEA-Ghana	Institute of Economic Affairs - Ghana
IEBL	Inter-Entity Boundary Line (Bosnia and Herzegovina)
IEC	Independent Electoral Commission (South Africa)
IECI	Independent Electoral Commission of Iraq
IFE	Instituto Federal Electoral (Mexico)
IFES	International Foundation for Electoral Systems
IFOR	Implementation Force (Bosnia and Herzegovina)
IGO	Inter-Governmental Organization
IMF	International Military Forces
IOM	International Organization for Migration
IPCC	Inter-party Consultative Committee (Liberia)
IPOA	International Peace Operations Association
IPI	International Peace Institute

IPTF	International Police Task Force (Bosnia and Herzegovina)
IRI	International Republican Institute
ISF	International Security Force
JEMB	Joint Elections Management Body (Afghanistan)
JEMBS	Joint Elections Management Body Secretariat (Afghanistan)
JEMBS ESU	Joint Elections Management Body Secretariat Election Security Unit (Afghanistan)
JEOC	Joint Elections Operations Center
JEST	Joint Elections Security Taskforce (Kosovo)
JPMC	Joint Political-Military Commission (Angola)
JOC	Joint Operations Centers
KFOR	Kosovo Force
KPS	Kosovo Police Service
MILF	Moro Islamic Liberation Front (Philippines)
MMU	Media Monitoring Unit (Guyana)
MNC-I	Multinational Corps-Iraq
NATO	North Atlantic Treaty Organization
NDI	National Democratic Institute
NEC	National Electoral Commission (Somaliland)
NPC	National Peace Council (Ghana)
OAS	Organization of American States
OSCE	Organization for Security and Cooperation in Europe
PERP	Preparation of Electoral Roll with Photographs Project
PMSC	Private Military and Security Companies
PPRC	Political Parties' Registration Commission (Sierra Leone)
QRF	Quick Reaction Forces
RTLM	Radio Television Libre des Milles Collines (Rwanda)
STV	Single Transfer Vote
SOP	Standard Operating Procedures
TSE	Supreme Electoral Council
UN	United Nations
UNCIVPOL	United Nations Civilian Police
UNDP	United Nations Development Programme
UNITA	Uniao Nacional para a Independencia Total de Angola
USAID	U.S. Agency for International Development
USG	United States Government
USIP	U.S. Institute for Peace
ZANU PF	Zimbabwe African National Union Patriotic Front

ANNEX III - SOURCES

ACE Electoral Knowledge Network – www.aceproject.org

Ajayi, Ola, Appeal Court sacks Senator Omisore, Vanguard, October 29, 2009

An, Mary, Programme Analyst, Governance and Rule of Law – Elections Support, UNDP, Sudan – Khartoum Office, interviewed October 28, 2009, interviewed on October 28, 2009

Bailey, Michael, Election Security Advisor, United National Mission in Haiti, interview: October 29, 2009

BBC News, Ivory Coast old foes 'rearming' October 29, 2009

BBC News, The Growing Power of Nigeria's Gangs, February 17, 2007

Bekoe, Dorina, Senior Research Associate (Africa), Center for Conflict Analysis and Prevention, United States Institute for Peace, interviewed on October 6, 2009

Beinhart, Eric, Associate Director, ICITAP, US Department of Justice, currently on detail as a Senior Criminal Justice Advisor, USAID DC Office, interviewed on October 26, 2009

Bjornlund, Eric, Beyond Free and Fair – Monitoring Elections and Building Democracy, Woodrow Wilson International Center for Scholars, 2004

Carothers, Thomas, Confronting the Weakest Link – Aiding Political Parties in New Democracies, Carnegie Endowment for International Peace, Washington, D.C., 2006

Cockanye, James, Emily Speers Mears, Iveta Cherneva, Alison Gurin, Sheila Oveido and Dylan Yaeger, Beyond Market Force, A Feasibility Study for a Standards Implementation and Enforcement Framework for the Global Security Industry

Collier, Paul, Wars, Guns, and Votes – Democracy in Dangerous Places, HarperCollins, 2009

Council of Europe, European Commission for Democracy Through Law, Report on Media Monitoring During Election Observation Missions, March 31, 2004

Declaration of Principles for International Election Observation and Code of Conduct for International Election Observers

Department for International Development, Preventing Violent Conflict, 2007

Dobbins, James, Seth G. Jones, Keith Crane, and Beth Cole DeGrasse, The Beginner's Guide to Nation-Building, RAND Corporation, 2007

Erben, Peter, former Chief Electoral Officer, United Nations Assistance Mission in Afghanistan, (2005), and Senior Electoral Advisor, IFES, interviewed on October 20, 2009

Fischer, Jeff, Elections in Fragile States (under review by Princeton University for publication), 2008

Fischer, Jeff, Electoral Conflict and Violence – A Strategy for Study and Prevention, IFES, 2002

Fischer, Jeff, Haiti Election Security Recommendations, 2000

Fischer, Jeff, Inter-Office Memorandum, Security Planning for Registration and Elections, OSCE, January 13, 2001

The Ghanaian Journal, NDC constituency election turns violent, November 7, 2009

Gloor, Anne, Election Support, Section for Peace Security, Swiss Federal Department of Foreign Affairs, interviewed on October 8, 2009

Graham, Andrew, Preparing Police Services in Democratic Regimes to Support the Electoral Process: A Survey of Leading Practice

Guatemala Human Rights Commission, Drug Gangs Use Violence to Sway Guatemala Vote, August 4, 2007

Hansen, Thomas Obel, Political Violence in Kenya – A Study of Causes, Responses, and a Framework for Preventative Action, November 2009

International Center for Transitional Justice - http://www/ictj.org/en/tj/

International Foundation for Electoral Systems - http://www.ifes.org

International Foundation for Electoral Systems - http://www.electionguide.org

Issue Brief, Timor-Leste Armed Violence Assessment, Electoral Violence in Timor-Leste – Mapping Incidents and Responses, 2009

Kitasei, Yume, Blood on the Ballots: A Cross-National Study of Electoral Violence Since 1990, Senior Thesis, Woodrow Wilson School of Public and International Affairs, Princeton University, 2009

Lyons, Terrance, Globalization, Diaspora, and Conflict, Institute for Conflict Analysis and Resolution, George Mason University, January 2004

Lyons, Terrance, Post-Conflict Elections: War Termination, Democratization, and Demilitarizing Politics, Working Paper No. 20, Institute for Conflict Analysis and Resolution, George Mason University, February 2002

Maley, Michael, Senior Deputy Chief Electoral Officer (Operations and Computerization), Electoral Component, UNTAC (1993), interviewed on October 22, 2009

Mansfield, Edward and Jack Snyder, Electing to Fight – Why Emerging Democracies Go To War, Harvard University, 2005

Norris, Pippa, Electoral Engineering – Voting Rules and Political Behavior, Cambridge University Press, 2004

Operational Plan Outline for the Afghanistan Presidential Election in 2004, Joint Election Management Body

Operational Plan, Iraqi Council of Representatives Election, December 2005, Independent Electoral Commission of Iraq

Organization for Security and Cooperation in Europe, Election Security Plan, April 1996

Organization for Security and Cooperation in Europe, Registration and Election Plan, 2000

Pastor, Robert A., Mediating Elections, Journal of Democracy, January 1998

Petit, Denis, Resolving Election Disputes in the OSCE Area: Toward a Standard Election Dispute Monitoring System, 2000.

Principles of the Interagency Conflict Assessment Framework, July 15, 2008

Reilly, Ben and Andrew Reynolds, Electoral Systems and Conflict in Divided Societies, National Research Council, 1999

Reuters, ICC to consider request for Kenya investigation, November 6, 2009

Schuler, Ian, National Democratic Institute: SMS as a Tool in Election Observation, Innovations Journal, MIT Press, Spring 2008

Sisk, Timothy D., Elections in Fragile States: Between Voice and Violence, International Studies Association, 2008

Straus, Scott and Charlie Taylor, Democratization and Electoral Violence in Sub-Saharan Africa, 1990-2007, 2009

SW Radio Africa News, http://www.swradioafrica.com/news191009/zanu191009.htm, October 19, 2009

The Times of India, Was delimitation the trigger? New Delhi, June 2, 2007

United Nations, International Police Task Force, General Elections – Duties and Responsibilities for Local Police Commanders, Bosnia and Herzegovina, 1996

United Nations Development Programme, Elections and Conflict Prevention – A Guide to Analysis, Planning and Programming, 2009

United Nations Peacebuilding Commission, Strategic Framework for Peacebuilding in Guinea-Bissau, July 31, 2008

United Nations Peacebuilding Fund - http://www/unpbf.org/emergency.shtml

UN Peacebuilding Support Office, Briefing Paper on Local Governance and Democracy in Post-Conflict Sierra Leone, November 1, 2007

United States Agency for International Development (USAID), Conflict Management and Mitigation (CMM), Conducting a Conflict Assessment – Framework for Strategy and Program Development, 2005

USAID, CMM, Power Point Conflict Diagnosis: The Conflict Equation, undated.

USAID, Managing Assistance in Support of Political and Electoral Processes, Technical Publications Series, January 2000

USAID, Monitoring and Evaluation in Post-conflict Settings, 2006,

US Department of State, Transition Elections and Political Processes in Reconstruction and Stabilization Operations: Lessons Learned. Office of the Coordinator for Stabilization and Reconstruction, 2007, 19-20.

The Wall Street Journal, Drug-Cartel Links Haunt an Election South of the Border, July 3, 2009

Walker, Tjip, Theories of Change for Conflict Management and Mitigation: DRAFT, USAID CMM, 2010

ANNEX IV: END NOTES

[1] Sisk, 18
[2] Fischer, Elections in Fragile States, 71
[3] http://www.aceproject.org
[4] Fischer, Elections in Fragile States, 73
[5] Sisk, 7
[6] DFID, 1
[7] Collier, 20 - 21
[8] UNDP, 5
[9] Straus and Taylor, 36 - 37
[10] Straus and Taylor, 26
[11] Lyons, Terrence, Globalization, Diasporas, and Conflict.
[12] Kitasei, 32.
[13] Sisk, 8
[14] Sisk, 2
[15] UNDP, 4
[16] Sisk, 16
[17] The Times of India, 19.
[18] UN Peacebuilding Support Office, 2
[19] UNDP, 10 - 11
[20] Kitasei, 18
[21] Kitasei, 36
[22] Kitasei, 20
[23] Issue Brief, 3-4
[24] Lyons, 29-30
[25] http://www.aceproject.org
[26] Straus and Taylor, 9 - 11
[27] Sisk, pages 14 - 16; UNDP, 19 - 22
[28] Fischer, Elections in Fragile States, 27-31.
[29] Bjornlund, 40
[30] USAID Managing Assistance in Support of Political and Electoral Processes, 18.
[31] UNDP, 26.
[32] Fischer, p. 32.
[33] US Department of State, 19-20
[34] USAID Managing Assistance in Support of Political and Electoral Processes, 51.
[35] Ibid, p. 52.
[36] UNDP, 61 - 63
[37] Graham, 18
[38] http://www.aceproject.org
[39] Ajayi
[40] Hansen, 19
[41] http://www.ictj.org/en/tj/
[42] UNDP, 38 - 39
[43] Gloor
[44] UNDP, 42
[45] Petit, 16
[46] Petit, 19
[47] UNDP, 40-41
[48] Schuler
[49] UNDP, 43
[50] Performance Management Plan - refer to USAID ADS 203.3.3 – 203.3.5.
[51] Walker, 1
[52] Section draws from: 1) Guidance on Evaluating Conflict Prevention and Peacebuilding Activities: A Working Draft for Application Period, a joint paper of the DAC Network on Conflict, Peace and Development Cooperation and the DAC Network on Development Evaluation, OECD 2008. 2) Programming in High Threat Environment Training, USAID. 3) Crisis Response and Recovery Training – 5, USAID.
[53] USAID Monitoring and Evaluation in Post-conflict Settings, 2-6.
[54] This section draws from: 1) Transition Elections and Political Processes in Reconstruction and Stabilization Operations: Lessons Learned. A Guide for US Government Planners, Office of the Coordinator for Stabilization and Reconstruction, US Department of State, November 2007, p. 22. 2) Programming in High Threat Environment Training, USAID. 3) Crisis Response and Recovery Training – 5, USAID.
[55] USAID, CMM Conducting a Conflict Assessment, 8
[56] Ibid, 28
[57] USAID CMM Power Point, Conflict Diagnosis : The Conflict Equation
[58] UNDP, 20-21